Skills for Success for your fifth grader

Written by
Mary Beth Koeppel

Illustrations by
Diana Magnuson

Cover Photography by Anthony Nex of Anthony Nex Photography

Photo Credits: © 1997 Comstock, Inc.: pages 1, 8, 14, 26, 32, 38, 41, 43, 44, 49, 51, 52, 62, 63, 64, 65, 66

FS-23006 Skills for Success for Your Fifth Grader

Table of Contents

Introduction

Academic Skills

Social Skills

Home and School Cooperation

Rewards

Student Workbook

FS-23006 Skills for Success for Your Fifth Grader

The Fantastic Fifth Grader!

Parents wear many hats every day. Each one is equally important, but sometimes parents are nervous about wearing the hat of "teacher" for their child. The truth is that all day every day the invisible "teacher hat" is perched on your head, perhaps even on top of another hat you may be wearing at the moment! The joy of parenting comes with making the most of every opportunity to be your child's "teacher."

Parents can be nervous about performing the role of teacher because they are not sure what expectations or goals are realistic for their child at each level. This book is aimed at helping you understand, appreciate, and accentuate the learning that your child is ready to experience.

You were and still are your child's first and most important teacher. By becoming familiar with the skills a fifth grader needs, you can be more efficient and effective as you continue in that role.

Fifth graders have a fantastic drive to discover. They are at an exciting stage as they begin their journey from childhood to adolescence.

WHAT Are FIFTH Graders Like?

- They are **excited** about trying new and challenging activities.
- They are **committed** to their ideas, friends, and family.
- They are **independent**. They want to be in charge of their own decisions.
- They are becoming increasingly **responsible** in their thoughts and deeds.
- They are **competitive**. They want to do well and win.
- They are **inventive**. They can put ideas or items together in new and creative ways.
- They are **thoughtful**; even though the thoughts sometimes follow, rather than precede, the actions.
- They are **cautious** about looking or acting differently from their peers.
- They are **wonderful** and will delight you with both their naivité and maturity.
- They are **ready to learn and grow** with your direction and the ideas in this book.

The Keys to Using This Book

Be a Learner

Be ready to tell your child that you don't know something. A question from your child indicates interest in the topic, but you don't need to feel embarrassed if you don't know the answer. The important step is to help your child look for an answer.

Teach to the Moment

Remember that the best time to teach anything is the moment your child has expressed curiosity about it. If your child asks a question about the phases of the moon, try to provide information, look it up with him or her in a science book or encyclopedia, and watch the sky. If you have access to the Internet or a computer with a multimedia reference tool, use that to gain instant facts to share.

Teach Academic Skills

The first section of this book provides a guide for you that's full of activities that center around the topics fifth graders study in school. Use it to help your child better understand a topic that is being taught and to enhance the learning your child is doing at school. Use the background information and the ideas to provide enjoyable interaction with your child.

Teach Social Skills

The next section centers around social skills. Even the most intelligent child will be less successful in school without good personal skills. These interpersonal skills are critical for positive relationships to develop and for your child to feel worthwhile. Use this section to provide an approach to a problem or an opening to discuss a topic. With prior discussion about these vital skills, your child will have strategies to deal with concerns when they appear.

Promote Home and School Cooperation

The next section of the book gives you practical ideas for how to navigate home and school interaction on a daily basis. There are suggestions for organizing, communicating with the educational community, conferencing with teachers, and getting involved at school.

Give Praise

Included in the book are reward items. Use these to show your child that you are proud of his or her efforts. Children respond to positive reinforcement. Teachers know that the more specific the praise, the better. "Good job!" is great to hear, but more repeat performances come from phrases such as "You wrote that story so neatly that it is easy for me to read. That shows me you are proud of it, too!"

Give Practice

The final section consists of skill pages for your child. Use them to check on your child's understanding of the skill. Use them to provide individual practice for a skill. Use them to provide a chance for your child to demonstrate progress! If your child has difficulty, you may want to repeat an activity or choose a new approach to helping him or her master that skill.

Reading for Fifth Graders

By the fifth grade, most children have mastered the basic reading skills and the emphasis shifts from word recognition and word analysis to comprehension and literary skills, vocabulary building skills, and library and research skills.

COMPREHENSION SKILLS

Fifth graders will be exposed to a variety of study strategies for building comprehension. They may use the K-W-L method to chart what they *know*, what they *want* to know, and what they have *learned* from a selection. They will be asked to read to find specific information. They will work on developing increased skill with summarizing, notetaking, predicting outcomes, and comparing and contrasting elements in a single selection or several selections. They will be expected to recognize the basic story elements of plot, setting, mood, theme, characters, conflict resolution, and climax. They will arrive at a deeper understanding of their reading through an increased use of projects and open-ended questions (those requiring more than a one word answer) to demonstrate their comprehension. Finding evidence in a story to support their opinions will also receive greater emphasis.

LITERARY SKILLS

In comparing literary works, fifth graders will learn to use characterization, author's point of view, main ideas, figurative language such as exaggeration and idioms (popular expressions), and to look for the use of propaganda. They will begin to build an awareness of different author's writing styles and different genres of reading such as humor, mystery, fantasy, realistic fiction, or adventure. They will begin to relate literature to their own life.

LIBRARY AND RESEARCH SKILLS

Fifth graders will need to exhibit greater proficiency locating books, magazines, CDs, videos, and other materials through the library's filing system. They will learn to use the table of contents, the glossary, and the index of a book to locate specific information.

VOCABULARY BUILDING SKILLS

At this level children are taught to use clues in the text of their reading as well as common word endings and beginnings to figure out word meanings. Specialized vocabulary is also being developed through material covered in specific subject areas.

ENCOURAGING READING

Independent Reading

1. Read to your child!
2. Have your child read to you.
3. Take turns reading, by paragraph or by page.
4. Let your child subscribe to a magazine. (See p. 7.)
5. Have reading material available at home—magazines, newspapers, books.
6. Visit the library frequently.
7. Let your child apply for his or her own library card.
8. Provide your child with books from bookstores, rummage sales, school book orders, book exchanges, and as gifts.
9. Provide your child with a special place to store personal books—bookshelf, bookrack, table, drawer, basket.
10. Encourage your child to read to younger siblings, cousins, or neighbors.
11. Purchase age-appropriate word puzzle books.
12. Let your child see you read. Portray yourself as a reader.
13. Share what you are reading.
14. Have a quiet time for family reading.
15. Help your child find books related to his or her special interests.
16. Don't limit reading to books. (See next idea *A Rose by Any Other Name*.)
17. Clip and share interesting articles or cartoons from the newspaper.
18. Create a family reading list on which all family members can record the books they have read.

At this level your child will be expected to select and complete a set amount of independent reading. Individual or class goals may be set specifying the amount of reading to be completed in number of books, number of pages, or number of minutes. Try the techniques on this page to motivate your child to read independently.

A Rose by Any Other Name

It is important to recognize that reading comes in many different forms. Although not all forms can be classified as great classical works of literature, they can all offer the benefits of improved comprehension and vocabulary skills. Here are some atypical reading materials that you may want to encourage your child to read: recipes, greeting cards, comics, song lyrics, CD/cassette cases, department store and specialty catalogs, parts catalogs and repair manuals, owner's manuals, driver's manuals, bumper stickers, game instructions and rules, assembly directions, advertisements, sale flyers, pamphlets, travel brochures, menus, placemats in restaurants, cereal boxes, road signs, and road maps. Look around you. Can you find any others?

READING ACTIVITIES

> You know the books are out there, but how do you find what is suitable for your child?

Booktalks

Parents and educators are continually searching for ways to get young readers to view reading as an adventure, entertainment, and comfort—a treasure, rather than a dreadful chore. This is where booktalks come in. A booktalk involves sharing a glimpse of a good book with an individual or group to lure them into wanting to read the book themselves. It involves summarizing the plot or relaying a funny or intriguing incident from the book to capture the listener's interest, but coming to a halt at a crucial point, never giving away the ending. You and your child may want to exchange booktalks from time to time. You may even want to include other parents and friends of your child and start a booktalk group. Of course, this will mean that you will have to read selections appropriate for your child's age in order to give a good booktalk. But that's OK because it is a good idea to be familiar with what your child is reading anyway.

Choosing Books for Children

Often children at this age get in a rut and continually choose books from one series to read. It is wonderful that they are reading, but as a parent you may want to introduce them to other authors or types of reading.

Many magazines dealing with family life and raising children will include a section of book recommendations including a short synopsis of each, as well as a suggested age. Often these articles refer only to the newer selections. For very extensive listings, make a visit to your public library. The children's section of the library should have numerous volumes devoted to choosing books for children. Not only will you find books that give general listings of the best books for children, but there will also be books that address special needs and will suggest books for gifted children, reluctant readers, children who speak English as a second language, or children who have physical handicaps. Other volumes will address specific topics such as non-sexist children's books or books to help children cope with separation and loss. There are also books listing award-winning children's books, such as those receiving the Newbery Award. Your library may even offer free pamphlets with lists of suggested titles by grade level.

The following pages contain titles of books and magazines that may appeal to your child.

GREAT BOOKS FOR FIFTH GRADERS

Folklore, Myths, Legends

Book of Greek Myths by Ingri and Edgar Parin D'Aulaire (Doubleday, 1962)
Camelot edited by Jane Yolen (Philomel, 1995)
Cut From the Same Cloth: American Women of Myth, Legend, and Tall Tale by Robert D. San Souci (Philomel, 1993)
Four Ancestors: Stories, Song, and Poems From Native North America told by Joseph Bruchac (BridgeWater, 1996)

Fiction

Blubber by Judy Blume (Bradbury, 1974)
Bridge to Terabithia by Katherine Paterson (HarperCollins, 1977)
The Chronicles of Narnia by C.S. Lewis (Macmillan, 1950–1956)
The Hundred Dresses by Eleanor Estes (Harcourt, 1944)
Island of the Blue Dolphins by Scott O'Dell (Houghton Mifflin, 1960)
My Side of the Mountain by Jean Craighead George (E. P. Dutton, 1959)
Pippi Longstocking by Astrid Lindgren (Viking, 1950)
The Pool Party by Gary Soto (Delacorte, 1993)
Sadako and the Thousand Paper Cranes by Eleanor Coerr (G. P. Putnam's, 1977)
Shiloh by Phyllis Reynolds Naylor (Atheneum, 1991)
The Watsons Go to Birmingham—1963 by Christopher Paul Curtis (Delacorte, 1995)

Poetry

Celebrate America in Poetry and Art edited by Nora Panzer (Hyperion, 1994)
Lunch Money and Other Poems About School by Carol Diggory Shields (Dutton, 1995)
A Pizza the Size of the Sun by Jack Prelutsky (Greenwillow, 1996)
Sad Underwear and Other Complications by Judith Viorst (Atheneum, 1995)
Sports Pages by Arnold Adoff (Lippincott, 1986)
You're Invited to Bruce Lansky's Poetry Party by Bruce Lansky (Meadowbrook, 1996)

Nonfiction

(Eyewitness Books) Seashore by Steve Parker (Knopf, 1989) [science/social studies series]
The Gettysburg Address illustrated by Michael McCurdy (Houghton Mifflin, 1995)
The I Hate Mathematics! Book by Marilyn Burns (Little, Brown, 1975)
(Inside the NFL) The Houston Oilers by Bob Italia (Abdo & Daughters, 1996) [series]
Incredible Comparisons by Russell Ash (Dorling Kindersley, 1996)
Janice VanCleave's The Human Body for Every Kid by Janice VanCleave (John Wiley, 1995) [science experiment series]
Kids Explore America's Hispanic Heritage by Westridge Young Writers Workshop (John Muir, 1992)
Kids With Courage: True Stories About Young People Making a Difference by Barbara A. Lewis (Free Spirit, 1992)
Leonardo Da Vinci by Diane Stanley (Morrow, 1996)
Lives of the Musicians: Good Times, Bad Times (and What the Neighbors Thought) by Kathleen Krull (Harcourt, Brace, Jovanovich, 1993)
We the People by Peter Spier (Doubleday, 1987)

Magazines for Fifth Graders

Just as adults enjoy reading short, timely, and interesting articles, kids do too. Look for these magazines at your local library or newsstand or let your child choose one to subscribe to.

Literature:

Cricket Magazine

Plays

Social Studies:

Cobblestone: The History Magazine for Young People

National Geographic World

Jr. Scholastic

Time for Kids

Science:

3-2-1 Contact

Kids Discover

Odyssey

Owl: The Discovery Magazine for Kids

Ranger Rick

Zoobooks

Art:

Crayola Kids

Pack-O-Fun

Physical Education:

Sports Illustrated for Kids

General Interest:

American Girl

Boys Life (Boy Scouts of America)

Disney Adventures

Highlights for Children

Mad

Zillions: for Kids From Consumer Reports

Read to Your Child

Read to your child, no matter what his or her age or ability! It is such a simple thing that you can do for your child, but it offers so many benefits. Not only is it enjoyable, entertaining, and relaxing, it stimulates the imagination more so than the same story on TV or video. It sharpens listening skills vital to your child's success in all areas of school and models good expression. It exposes your child to new vocabulary which he or she will then be more readily able to read independently.

For a reluctant reader, it can build positive feelings towards reading. Hearing a portion of a book orally may be all the incentive your child needs to go on and finish the book. Children can often understand material that is more advanced than their own reading ability. This is especially true if your child is reading below grade level. By reading aloud, you are not limiting your child only to the information and the enjoyment of books he or she can read independently.

Don't be afraid to read to your child from books that would be classified as adult fiction or non-fiction if it covers a topic that would be of interest to your child. The series by James Herriot starting with *All Creatures Great and Small* would be an excellent choice for a child interested in animals. Or read favorite parts of a classic like *Treasure Island* by Robert Louis Stevenson to your child in conjunction with his or her reading of a children's abridged version.

Motivate With Tapes

Using a tape recorder can offer many ways to motivate reading.

* Books on tape are available from most libraries. Listen to some with your child. They are especially handy on long car trips.
* Try making some tapes for your child. Tape the first few chapters of a book you think he or she might enjoy or several exciting chapters from an old favorite. Don't be afraid to be very dramatic.
* Let your child record himself or herself reading aloud a favorite story or chapter. Suggest sending the tape to a grandparent, aunt, uncle, or cousin. Maybe they'll pick up on the idea and send one back. (Especially with a bit of encouragement from you!)

Video Versions

Look for videos that dramatize familiar children's books. Suggest that your child read the book before or after watching the video. Help your child to compare the two versions. Ask which your child preferred and why. These are some titles you may want to look for:

Babe, the Gallant Pig by Dick King-Smith
The Best Christmas Pageant Ever by Barbara Robinson
The Borrowers by Mary Norton
Charlotte's Web by E. B. White
The Indian in the Cupboard by Lynne Reid Banks
Matilda by Roald Dahl
Old Yeller by Fred Gipson
Sarah, Plain and Tall by Patricia MacLachlan
The Secret Garden by Frances H. Burnett
Sounder by William Armstrong
Stone Fox by John Reynolds Gardiner

Tune In to Trading Cards

If your child has a collection of trading cards for favorite sports figures, you can use them to strengthen important reading skills. Read the cards with your child. He or she may be more willing to read in this informal context. Then help your child apply the commonly used study strategy below in comparing and contrasting favorite players.

Use a Venn Diagram to compare and contrast two favorite sports figures. Draw two intersecting, or overlapping, circles and label one for each of the two players. Write facts that are true for both players in the area where the two circles overlap. Write information that is only true for one of the players in the part of the circle that is his or hers alone. Try this for several pairs of players. Look for the two players with the most in common. Explain to your child that this is a good way to remember facts about the players.

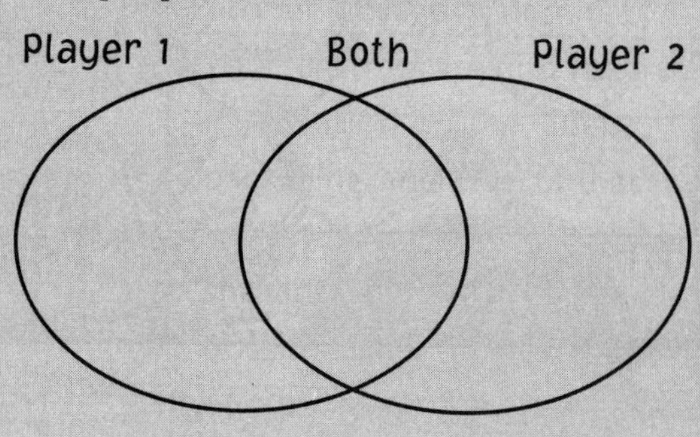

MORE READING ACTIVITIES

The newspaper can be a fabulous motivational tool. Since many newspapers are actually written at a fifth- or sixth-grade level, this would be an ideal time to introduce it to your child (if you haven't already done so).

Great News!

- Point out the different sections into which the paper is divided.
- Give your child tips on how to skim the paper for topics of interest to him or her.
- Look for an index to see which features it lists.
- Suggest that your child flip through a section reading headlines until one catches the eye.
- Explain how your child can get a summary of an article's content by reading the first line, or lead, which generally answers five questions: who, what, when, where, and why.
- Find and read the comics. Ask your child which strips appeal to kids.
- Search for articles or standings that correspond to your child's favorite teams or sports.

Together you can take your cue from items you find in the paper and participate in events covered, experiment with recipes and household projects, visit places, or even write letters to the editor or to the advice column. However you choose to use it, the newspaper offers current information on a variety of topics and is sure to fuel the curiosity of your child.

Positive Television

Article after article continues to crop up in just about every parenting, family, and educational magazine expounding the harmful effects of television in our children's lives. Still, it is highly unlikely that this multi-million dollar enterprise will ever be eliminated. With this in mind, we would do well to look for positive ways to put it to work. One such positive application would be to use your child's favorite shows to familiarize him or her with the basic story elements. After all, television has mastered the art of resolving any conflict, large or small, in 30 minutes, minus commercials. Your child should already be familiar with the setting and the characters. The theme, mood, and conflict of the show are established early due to the strict time constraints. Your child may learn to recognize the climax as that tense moment just before they cut to the last commercial and the conflict resolution as the happy ending where everything falls neatly into place in the final moments before the credits roll.

Fascinating Facts

Children at this age are often mesmerized by fascinating facts, lists, and records. If this is the case with your child, expose him or her to resources like *The Guiness Book of World Records, Famous First Facts, Information Please Almanac*, and *The Book of Lists*. All of these and many others are available at your public library.

Biographies

Visit your local library and help your child find additional reading on people and events of special interest to him or her. This will help to familiarize your child with library skills and different types of reading other than fiction.

Encyclopedia Search

Your child can complete page 73 to practice locating information in an encyclopedia. Many schools and families now use CD-ROM encyclopedias with their computers. If you have one, help your child practice locating any of the topics from that page using the search features of your software.

Mystery Word

Here is a game for sharpening dictionary skills and critical thinking skills. One person thinks of a word and gives a clue about its category—color word, action, school object, part of the body, and so on. Other players have to try to guess the word. The only further information the first player can give, however, is whether the guessed word comes before or after the mystery word in the alphabet. It is up to the players to think of a strategy for narrowing down their choices.

Parts of a Book

Gather a variety of nonfiction books including textbooks. Skim through them together to discover features they have that help a reader find or better understand information:

* title page
* copyright page (date may be important if you need current facts)
* table of contents
* chapter or unit titles
* subheadings
* glossary (defines words at back of book)
* bibliography (cites resources used)
* index

Being familiar with these parts of a book will help your child when he or she goes to do research for a report.

VOCABULARY ACTIVITIES

Get to the Root

Use a diagram of a plant like the one shown here to illustrate the concept of root words. Write a Latin or Greek root and its meaning "below ground." Think of words that contain the root. Write them on leaves to make a plant. Start with these roots. Which makes the largest plant?

Root	Meaning
aqua	water
cept	take
cred	believe
dent	tooth
ped	foot
phon	sound
rupt	break
scri	write
therm	heat
vis	see

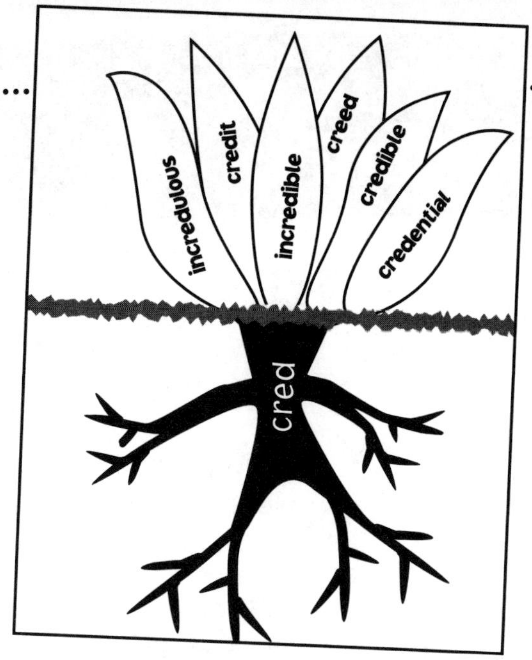

Learn Some New Words

Think of a few categories, such as "read it," "ride it," and "live in it." Then list several challenging words to match. Have your child guess which category each would fit into and then look up the words in a dictionary to check. Here are examples for each category listed above:

itinerary	yacht	chateau
novel	chariot	bungalow
eulogy	carousel	dormitory
agenda	stallion	kibbutz

Instead of "Said"

How many words can you and your child brainstorm that can be used instead of "said"? This exercise will help your child to write more interesting conversation.

The "Nyms"

Synonyms—two or more words with the same or nearly the same meaning (Example: silly, ludicrous)

Antonyms—words with opposite meanings (Example: sad, content)

Homonyms—two or more words that are pronounced the same but have different spellings and meanings (Example: braid, brayed)

Here are three activities you may want to do involving "nyms":

- Take turns thinking of pairs of synonyms, antonyms, or homonyms. Your "opponent" must think of a sentence that uses both words in the pair.
- Take turns thinking of a sentence using only one of a pair of synonyms, antonyms, or homonyms. Spell aloud the one used. Your partner then gives a sentence using the other word in the pair and must also spell it correctly.
- Choose a word like *residence, vehicle, large,* or *pretty* and see how many other words you and your child can think of that are similar in meaning. When you run out of ideas, use a thesaurus to add to the list.

Language Arts for Fifth Graders

Language Arts deals with all forms of communication. It covers writing, speaking, listening, and the use of proper grammar and spelling.

WRITING

As a fifth grader, your child will be exposed to a variety of writing forms including expressive, imaginative, informative, and persuasive. Fifth graders are challenged to demonstrate their ability to produce a written product through a variety of writing experiences.

Grammar and Mechanics

Most likely your child will be taught parts of speech, sentence construction, capitalization, and punctuation through the context of creative writing. For example, a teacher might do a mini-skills lesson on adjectives and then encourage students to focus on descriptive words in their writing.

Spelling

Fifth-grade spelling is much more involved than memorizing spelling lists. Your child should be able to use a variety of sources besides the dictionary to find correct spellings. These sources include books, magazines, personal word books, adults, peers, and even a computer spell check. Fifth graders are expected to correctly spell a broader base of words in their writing. They will be given experience in editing and revising their work for spelling errors. At this level, spelling often becomes more meaningful when lists are drawn from content areas.

Penmanship

By fifth grade, most of your child's writing will be in cursive. Although your child will have already received instruction in how to write in cursive in previous years, he or she will continue to be monitored for improvement of handwriting techniques. There are several accepted cursive styles. It will be necessary for you to identify the one taught in your child's school.

SPEAKING

Your child will be given more opportunities to exhibit verbal skills through a greater variety of speaking experiences. He or she will learn about the use of facial expressions, gestures, voice inflections, rate and volume of delivery, and use of eye contact for more effective speaking.

LISTENING

Your fifth grader will find that besides listening for directions and factual information, he or she will be expected to recognize a speaker's purpose, make inferences from what is said, and summarize and sequence spoken information. Your child may learn ways to organize spoken language through different note-taking strategies.

A Shared Journal

Journals and learning logs have become very popular learning tools in recent years. They encourage daily writing in a nonthreatening format on subjects that are familiar to students. Modeling writing for students is another positive technique used in classrooms. You can combine these two activities to arrive at a very worthwhile learning activity for you and your child.

Using a plain spiral notebook, begin a Shared Journal. Take turns with your child making entries in this journal. Entries may be very simple, consisting of only a few lines. The topics are unlimited. You may want to comment on what you did while your child was at school, something that made you particularly happy or sad during the day, or something you are planning to do in the near or distant future. You could recall a past event that you shared with your child or take the opportunity to praise your

child for some task he or she worked hard at or performed well. Begin each entry with a date which will make your journal more meaningful when looking back over your entries in the future. You may want to establish certain times for each of you to make your entries. You may want to write after your child has gone to bed, leaving the journal for your child to read in the morning. Your child may choose to write an entry before leaving for school, while on a long bus ride, or while you prepare dinner.

The Perfect Postcard

Cut tagboard or any other white lightweight cardboard into rectangles the size of postcards. Have your child depict family outings and activities in marker or colored pencil on one side. On the other side, have your child write a brief description of the event followed by a short personal message. Be sure and leave room on the right for an address and postage as on an actual postcard. Help your child address this specialized postcard to a favorite friend or relative and actually mail it.

This activity will not only benefit your child's reading and writing by giving him or her meaningful opportunities to do both, but can serve as a valuable communication tool between you and your child.

MORE WRITING ACTIVITIES

Mad About Mail

Children of all ages enjoy receiving their own mail. Use this simple pleasure to give your child reading practice. Write letters to your child and mail them from work or shopping. In time your child may want to start answering your letters. A renewed interest in reading will be well worth the cost of postage.

Celebrity Mail

Your child may enjoy writing letters to favorite authors, TV stars, singers, or sports figures and will often be surprised to actually receive responses, even if some of them are "form" responses. (Your child will have a better chance of getting a reply if he or she includes a stamped, self-addressed envelope.) This activity may take a bit of detective work in locating addresses. You may have luck checking your library information desk and fan magazines, which will further benefit your child by sharpening research skills.

E-Mail

If you have a computer and Internet access, you may want to encourage your child to write letters using electronic mail, or e-mail as it's commonly called. E-mail is a great way to communicate with friends and relatives who live in another city, state, or country.

Now That's Poetry!

Where the Sidewalk Ends by Shel Silverstein (Harper & Row, 1974) contains some fabulous poetry for reading aloud that is sure to tickle the funnybone. You may want to encourage your child to write his or her own poetry modeled after some of the poems you have read in this book. For example, after reading aloud "Invention," your child could try and think of his or her own invention with its own unique problem. Or try reading "It's Dark in Here" and follow it up with a personal poem offering an excuse for poor handwriting. (We all need one at one time or other!)

You Are Cordially Invited to . . .

Look through magazines for pictures of interesting events. Write invitations to match. If you have a computer, your child might enjoy trying out creative fonts to make sophisticated or fun invitations.

GRAMMAR

Parts of Speech

Fifth graders usually focus on these parts of speech:

Nouns—name a person, place, or thing (Examples: child, library, rock)

Pronouns—take the place of nouns (Examples: I, you, she, it, him, us)

Verbs—are action words or a form of "be" (Examples: go, think, skated, am, is, were)

Adjectives—describe nouns and pronouns (Examples: red, quiet, hungry, round)

Adverbs—describe verbs, adjectives, or other adverbs; tell how, when, or where; often end in *-ly* (Examples: happily, quickly, very, more)

Speech-egories

One person chooses a letter of the alphabet and the other chooses one of these four parts of speech—noun, verb, adjective, or adverb. Set a timer for one to three minutes. Each person writes as many words as possible beginning with that letter that are the chosen part of speech. The person with the longest list wins.

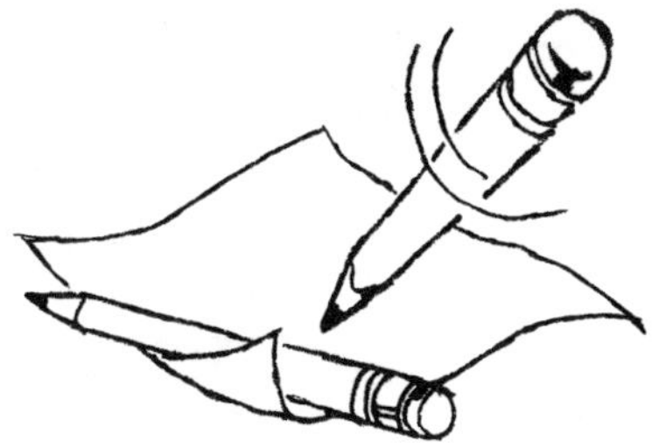

TIME CAPSULE
Mom's fudge recipe
Dad's jokes
Ben's Packer jersey
Marty's marbles

Parts-of-Speech Scramble

Think of three examples each for these parts of speech—noun, verb, adjective, and adverb. Write them on separate slips of paper and scramble them up. Have your child sort the slips by part of speech. Next have your child choose one slip from each pile and combine them to form silly sentences. (It works best if the nouns you choose are plural nouns.) Point out that the adjective precedes the noun and the noun precedes the verb, but the adverb can be correctly used in several positions.

Our Family's Time Capsule

Children of all ages often confuse the formation of plurals and the formation of possessives. Plurals mean "more than one" and regular plurals are formed by adding s to a noun. Possessives show ownership. Singular possessives are formed by adding apostrophe s ('s) to a noun. To give practice with possessives, help your child write a family or class time capsule. The time capsule should be a list that tells what item belonging to each family member or classmate would be included.

Example:

Nouns	Verbs	Adjectives	Adverbs
teachers	scream	small	tomorrow
monsters	practice	green	softly
musicians	run	horrible	forcefully

Green monsters scream forcefully.

Forcefully, green monsters scream.

Green monsters forcefully scream.

Addressing an Envelope

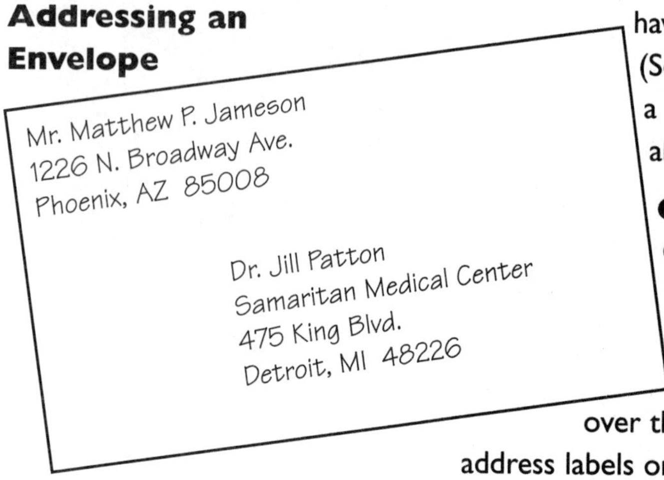

Here are some common rules of capitalization and punctuation your child should know regarding names and addresses:

- All titles begin with a capital letter.
- Abbreviations for titles end with a period.
- Names of people begin with a capital letter.
- Initials are capitalized and followed by a period.
- Names of places (businesses, streets, cities, states) begin with capital letters.
- Words such as road, street, lane, and boulevard are capitalized when used in an address, even when abbreviated. Abbreviations for these words end with a period.
- The city and state are separated by a comma.
- Postal abbreviations for states are made of two capital letters. They do not have a period. (See page 35 for a listing of postal abbreviations.)

Getting a Good Return

Have your child look over the return address labels on your daily mail. Challenge him or her to tell you the matching rules for each capital letter, punctuation mark, or abbreviation used or to catch any errors in the return addresses.

A Capital Idea

Make a list of family doctors, dentists, neighbors, teachers, religious leaders, and civic leaders familiar to your child. Include titles, initials for the first names, and full words for the last names, but do not use capital letters or punctuation. Have your child rewrite the list using correct capitalization and punctuation.

Telephone Time

Supply your child with a telephone book, paper, and a pencil. Have your child pick out interesting names and addresses and rewrite them using the correct capitalization and punctuation. This makes a good punctuation drill because although capitals are used, punctuation is usually omitted in telephone directories. Have your child see how many different abbreviations he or she can find. Or give your child specific things to look for, such as these:

Find the name and address of a doctor.

Find an address of someone who lives on a boulevard.

Find the name and address of someone who uses two initials.

Find three addresses of people with your first name.

Find names and addresses that include the first name of each person in your family.

SPELLING

Sticky Spelling

Self-sticking notes are readily available in a great variety of sizes, colors, and designs from business supply stores to discount stores. Have your child write his or her spelling words on separate notes and stick them in conspicuous places around the home. Throughout the week, encourage your child to stop, look at, and spell these words every time he or she comes across one.

Crosswords

Have your child arrange all the week's spelling words in a crossword puzzle. Challenge your child to connect all the words in one puzzle if possible. Working with the words will help to reinforce the spellings for your child. This activity can be done on a regular sheet of writing paper. If your child is having difficulty aligning the words, it may be helpful to supply him or her with graph paper.

Turnabout Is Fair Play

Suggest that your child give you a spelling test of the assigned list of words. The test can be oral or written. Either will require that your child pay close attention to the words to determine whether you are providing the correct spelling, with the added pleasure of trying to catch you in a spelling error.

How Does This Compute?

Help your child as needed in typing his or her spelling list on the computer. Use the format commands to enlarge the words for easier reading and then print the list. Typing the words and seeing them in enlarged print will help to reinforce the spellings. This will also provide your child with a clear list from which to do further studying and may be particularly helpful for children with poor handwriting.

Riddle Me

Take turns making up riddles about the words on your child's spelling lists. The riddles should draw attention to the word's spelling more so than its meaning. Clues may point out such things as double consonants, word endings, small words within the word, words with similar spellings, number of vowels or consonants, or how many different vowels. Both making up and solving the riddles will help to reinforce the spellings for your child in a more enjoyable way.

Let's Play a Game

Many familiar commercial games are based on the use of spelling skills and can be played to help strengthen your child's proficiency. These include games such as Spill and Spell, Boggle, Scrabble, and Upwords. In using these games, feel free to adapt the rules to make them more closely match your child's ability level. For example, in Scrabble and Upwords you may want to sit so that all players can view other players' tiles and offer suggestions for possible words.

Scrambled Letters

You may on occasion wish to use the letter tiles from a commercial game as study tools without actually playing the game. (Magnetic letters work well for this idea, too.) Gather the letters in one of your child's spelling words, scramble them, and allow time for your child to arrange them in the correct order. While your child is unscrambling one word, you can be finding the letters for the next.

Spelling for Sale

The next time you are browsing the aisles of your favorite grocery store, have your child play detective and look for names of familiar products that have been purposely misspelled for advertising purposes. Invite your child to make a list of these in a small notebook with the correct spelling written next to the incorrect version.

Add a Letter

Try this spelling challenge game to pass time while driving, cooking, or waiting for appointments. Or squeeze a round in during a commercial break or while getting ready for bed. The first player thinks of a word and without disclosing the word, gives the first letter. The second player gives a second letter. If it is not the second letter of the word that the first player was originally thinking of, the first player must then think of another word that begins with those two letters instead and supply the third letter. Play passes back and forth in this manner until a word is spelled. The person supplying the last letter of the word (whatever it turns out to be) receives the point. It helps if players on their turn say all the previous letters before adding their new letter.

PENMANSHIP

These are two styles of cursive handwriting commonly used in schools. Check with your child's teacher to see which penmanship style is preferred.

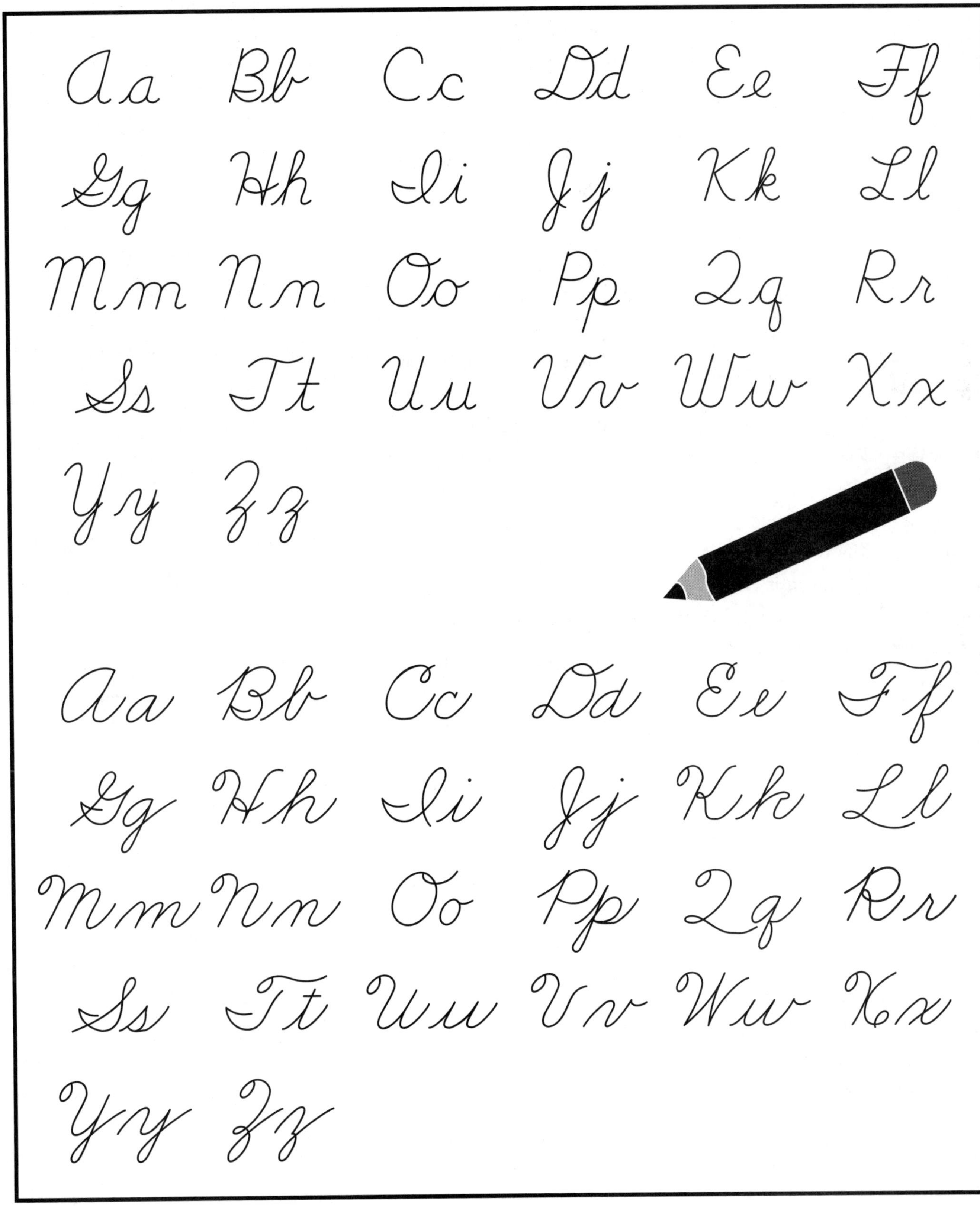

Doorway Puppet Theater

If you think your child would still enjoy dramatizing stories that he or she is reading through the use of puppetry, here is a simple way to make a puppet theater. Purchase a spring tension curtain rod that will fit snugly in a doorway of your home. Secure it in the doorway about four feet from the floor. Drape an afghan, bedsheet, or colorful fabric remnant over the rod. That's all it takes! The puppeteers take to one side and their audience is seated on the opposite side. Make simple puppets out of socks, paper bags, or drawings taped to popsicle sticks and let the show begin.

Story Boxes

Find an old shoebox and have your child decorate it if desired. Then select six common items from around your home or yard and place them in the box. Challenge your child to make up a story that somehow includes all six items. You may want to take turns building the story together. Change the items in the box frequently and repeat the activity.

Sing-along

You and your child may enjoy writing new lyrics for familiar tunes to liven up ordinary evenings or special events. Hand out copies of the new words to everyone present and get them all to join in.

Name That City

To help stimulate creative thinking, look over a state or U.S. map with your child. Pick out cities with unusual sounding names like Sandwich, Illinois, or Sylvester, Georgia, and together try to imagine how they got their names. This would make a great activity for passing the time on a long car trip using maps in the car and signs along the road.

Telephone Time

Giving your child the opportunity to answer the phone and take accurate messages can give him or her experience with speaking, listening, and writing. Begin by suggesting appropriate ways to answer the phone and clarifying what information your child should and should not give out over the phone. Detail the information you would like your child to get from a caller, such as name, phone number, and a brief message. Role play the activity before putting your child on the spot. You may also want to let your child make calls to stores and other businesses for you when you need simple information such as store hours.

Math for Fifth Graders

At the fifth-grade level, the math concepts will continue to build on what was covered in previous years. Continued drill and practice of basic facts and operations (+ – x ÷) will give your child a strong foundation for new material introduced.

As in previous years, emphasis will be on learning strategies for problem solving. At this level, problems will often require more than one step. Showing your child how math concepts branch into almost all areas of life is very important.

PLACE VALUE AND NUMBER SENSE

- Reading and writing numbers in the billions
- Rounding numbers
- Comparing and ordering whole numbers (Example: 32,074 > 31,999)

OPERATIONS

- Two-digit by three-digit multiplication
- Dividing by two-digit numbers

TIME AND MONEY

- Problem solving involving adding and subtracting time
- Adding, subtracting, multiplying, and dividing money

DECIMALS AND FRACTIONS

- Reading and writing numbers to the thousandths place (Example: 0.508)
- Converting between decimals, fractions, and percentages (Example: 0.5 = ½ = 50%)
- Writing fractions and mixed numbers (Example: 3⅘)
- Adding, subtracting, multiplying, and dividing fractions
- Writing ratios (Example: *3 books : 1 child*)

MEASUREMENT

- Estimating and measuring length, weight, and capacity in both the U.S. customary units and metric units

GEOMETRY

- Identifying and constructing 2-D and 3-D figures
- Using a compass and protractor to measure and draw figures
- Calculating perimeter (distance around a figure), area (space inside a 2-D figure), and volume (space inside a 3-D figure)

Estimation Without Hesitation

Try some household estimating. Choose common items such as chairs, windows, doors, rooms, or lights. Family members make an estimate of how many you could find in your home. Then send your child off to make an actual count. Some other items to estimate might include doorknobs, cereal boxes, pairs of shoes, towels—well the list could go on and on and get sillier and sillier.

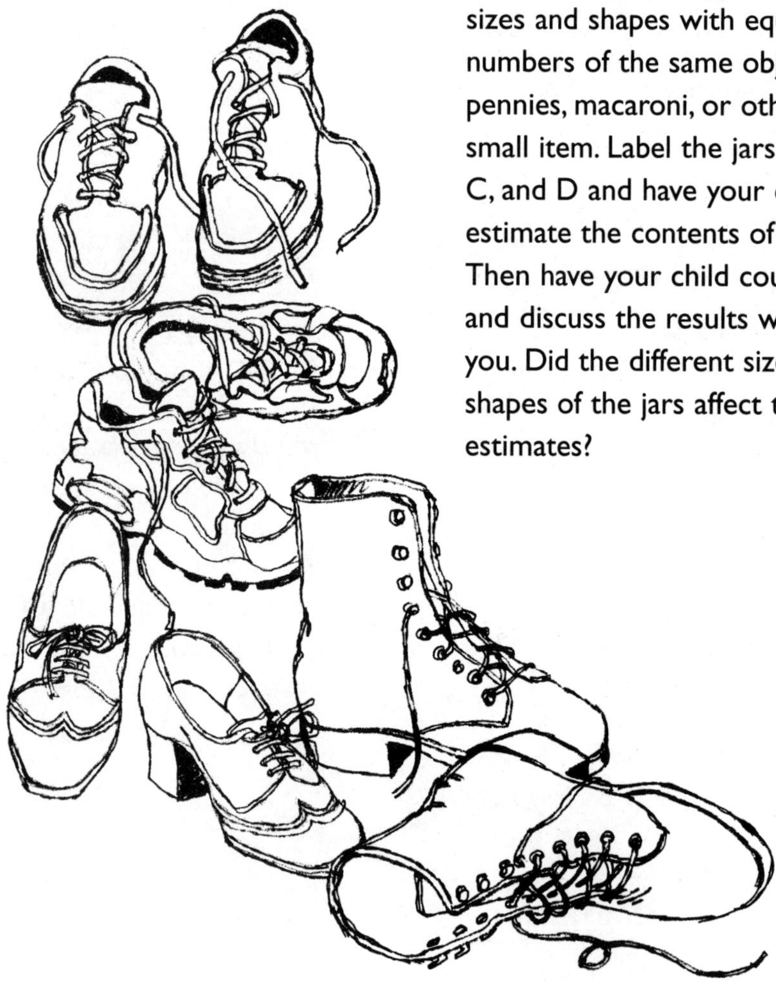

What's in the Jar?

Fill four jars of different sizes and shapes with equal numbers of the same object—pennies, macaroni, or other small item. Label the jars A, B, C, and D and have your child estimate the contents of each. Then have your child count and discuss the results with you. Did the different sizes and shapes of the jars affect the estimates?

How Much Is a Million?

The picture book *How Much Is a Million?* by David Schwartz (Lothrop, Lee & Shepard, 1985) is designed to introduce children to big numbers like a million, a billion, and a trillion. Your fifth grader may enjoy reading the author's note at the back of the book where he explains how he calculated comparisons, such as a billion kids making a human tower would stretch past the moon.

Invite your child to draw or describe comparisons to help explain these numbers: 100; 1,000; 10,000; 100,000; and 1,000,000.

MATH FUN AND GAMES

Count to 20 With a Twist

The object of this simple number game is to try and force your opponent to reach 20 first. Alternate counting by ones. Players may say one or two numbers at their turn. This activity will help develop thinking skills.

Licensed For Math

Try this challenge game on your next road trip! Each player picks a license plate on a passing car and adds, subtracts, or multiplies the numbers on the plate. The player with the highest answer wins the round. You may find yourself at a slight disadvantage on this one. As the driver, you will have to perform the math mentally while your child can use paper and pencil. Try aiming for the lowest answer in some rounds, also.

How Long?

Use a road atlas mileage chart to find the number of miles between your home and in-state or out-of-state places of interest. Help your child divide each distance by 30, 40, 50, and 60 to see how many hours it would take to reach each destination while travelling at these speeds.

Commercial Games

Numerous commercial games are available that deal with math and problem solving skills, such as Yahtzee, Racko, Triominoes, Mastermind, Battleship, Checkers, Chess, Uno, Chinese Checkers, Sorry, and Payday.

Magical Math

Children at this age are often fascinated by magic, especially if they can perform some of the magic themselves. You can use this interest to help your child build math skills, seeing as some magic simply applies math principles. For example, tell your child that you are going to guess the answer to a four-step math problem that he or she makes up. With your back turned, write 1,089 on a slip of paper and fold it. Then give your child the directions listed in the column on the right.

1. Write down any number with 3 different digits.

2. Reverse the digits and write the new number.

3. Subtract the smaller number from the larger one. (If the remainder has only 2 digits, put a 0 in the hundreds' place.)

4. Reverse the digits in the answer and add this number to the answer.

$$\begin{array}{r} 654 \\ -\,456 \\ \hline 198 \\ +\,891 \\ \hline 1{,}089 \end{array} \qquad \begin{array}{r} 897 \\ -\,798 \\ \hline 099 \\ +\,990 \\ \hline 1{,}089 \end{array}$$

Show your child the answer on your slip of paper and watch his or her surprise. Once you share the secret that the answer will always be 1,089, your child will be ready to go try it on a friend or the whole class!

MULTIPLICATION AND DIVISION CHART

This chart shows the multiplication and division problems your child should know accurately and instantly.

Multiplication:

factor x factor = product

3 x 4 = 12

4 x 3 = 12

Division:

dividend ÷ divisor = quotient

12 ÷ 3 = 4

12 ÷ 4 = 3

Basic Multiplication Facts

The basic facts are the 1-digit by 1-digit multiplication problems a child needs to learn in order to solve greater problems. This chart also includes problems involving 10, 11, and 12. These are valuable to know in order to solve everyday problems, such as working with dozens or converting inches to feet.

x	0	1	2	3	4	5	6	7	8	9	10	11	12
0	0	0	0	0	0	0	0	0	0	0	0	0	0
1	0	1	2	3	4	5	6	7	8	9	10	11	12
2	0	2	4	6	8	10	12	14	16	18	20	22	24
3	0	3	6	9	12	15	18	21	24	27	30	33	36
4	0	4	8	12	16	20	24	28	32	36	40	44	48
5	0	5	10	15	20	25	30	35	40	45	50	55	60
6	0	6	12	18	24	30	36	42	48	54	60	66	72
7	0	7	14	21	28	35	42	49	56	63	70	77	84
8	0	8	16	24	32	40	48	56	64	72	80	88	96
9	0	9	18	27	36	45	54	63	72	81	90	99	108
10	0	10	20	30	40	50	60	70	80	90	100	110	120
11	0	11	22	33	44	55	66	77	88	99	110	121	132
12	0	12	24	36	48	60	72	84	96	108	120	132	144

TIME AND MONEY

It's About Time

Here are a few time activities to try:

- ✷ While watching television, have your child keep track of how long a 30-minute program really is and how many minutes of commercials there are during that time segment.
- ✷ Record a starting time on a scrap of paper for any daily activity or errand, such as a meal time or a trip to the grocery store. Record the ending time also. Use subtraction to determine how long the activity took.
- ✷ Given the usual travel time and the expected time of arrival at a ballgame, dentist appointment, piano lesson, or school activity, have your child determine the latest time he or she can leave the house and still make it there on time.

Earn and Learn

Play the game on page 81 about earning and spending to give your child experience adding and subtracting money.

Sharp at Shopping

Shopping is another natural opportunity to sharpen math skills.

- ✷ As you choose items, ask your child to round the price to the nearest dollar. Then help your child keep a running total. See how close you can come to the actual total.
- ✷ If you are coupon shopping, give your child the challenge of subtracting the coupon amount from the price of the item to determine the new price.
- ✷ Encourage your child to help you compare prices. Explain how to divide the cost by the number of ounces to find the cost per ounce of an item. Do this for several items and determine which has the cheapest cost per ounce by comparing your answers. This division may be difficult for fifth graders, but it would be a great opportunity to give your child experience with a calculator. Some grocery stores even supply calculators on the shopping carts. Even if you need to help your child with the division, comparing decimals is an important skill at this level.

Score Big

Children love secret codes. Use this variation of a familiar code to give your child some valuable addition practice. Write the ABC's across the top of a sheet of paper. Have your child assign each letter a different amount in dollars or cents. Next write different names and words and add the corresponding money amounts to see how much each is worth. To make a game out of it, choose a category such as colors, animals, or foods. Set a timer and see who can find the most expensive word in that category within the time limit.

a	b	c	d	e	f	g	h	i
25¢	$1.10	60¢	95¢	20¢	$1.05	$1.00	75¢	50¢

fig = $1.05 + 50¢ + $1.00 = $2.55

beef = $1.10 + 20¢ + 20¢ + $1.05 = $2.55

GEOMETRY AND MEASUREMENT

Your child can get a better understanding of the idea of symmetry by using graph paper and markers or colored pencils.

Lines of Symmetry

Instruct your child to fold a piece of the graph paper in half. Using the markers, make an interesting design on half of the paper by coloring in different squares. Later, use the fold as the line of symmetry and try to color in the mirror image of the design on the opposite side of the fold.

Alphabet Symmetry

Look at printed capital letters. Try to determine which of the letters are symmetrical and which are not. Some may be symmetrical horizontally like D, some may be symmetrical vertically like A, and some are both like H.

A Geometry Hunt

A geometry activity that younger children enjoy is looking for familiar shapes like circles and rectangles in the environment around them. This would probably be too easy for this age group, but you may want to try sending your child in search of parallel, perpendicular, or intersecting lines.

Parallel lines are any two lines that are an equal distance apart at any point on the two lines.

Perpendicular lines are two lines that meet to form a right angle (90°), or square corner.

Intersecting lines are any two lines that cross at one point.

If your child enjoys this, try an angles search.

Right angles are 90°, or square.

Acute angles are less than 90°.

Obtuse angles are greater than 90°.

Guess That Height

Gather together a variety of measuring tools such as a ruler, a yardstick, and a tape measure. Choose different household items, such as tables, chairs, doorways, distance from floor or ceiling to a picture, windows, lamps, or curtains. Each person estimates the height of the objects. Then help your child decide which measuring device would be most suitable and measure the item. Compare your estimates to the actual height. Be sure to estimate and measure in both U.S. customary and metric units. **Variation:** Find some round or cylinder-shaped objects like canisters and estimate their circumference (distance around).

FRACTIONS AND DECIMALS

Pizza Pieces

Give your child experience with fractions the next time you have pizza, cake, or even meatloaf! Instruct your child to cut the food into sixths, eighths, or whatever would be suitable. Remind him or her that all pieces must be equal.

Munchable Math

Cooking with your child offers many opportunities to develop math skills. It provides practice in measuring and fractions. To make it even more challenging, choose a recipe that you can double, triple, or cut in half. This will give your child exposure to higher level fraction skills with built in rewards!

Who Uses Decimals?

Do a search through books, encyclopedias, almanacs, magazines, catalogs, newspapers, and other printed material to find examples of decimals. What are they used for? To which place (tenths, hundredths, thousandths) are they usually written?

To the Nearest Tenth

Have your child use a centimeter ruler with millimeter divisions to measure 10 everyday items to the nearest tenth of a centimeter.

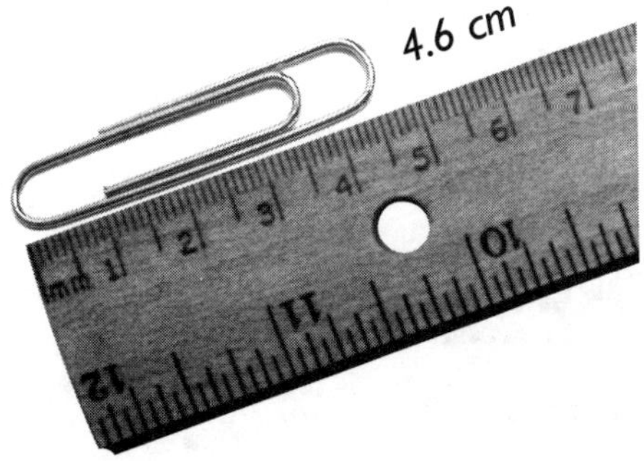

Sports Standings

Have your child look in the newspaper to find the standings of his or her favorite professional sports teams. Teach your child that winning percentages are shown in decimal form and are calculated by dividing the number of wins by the total number of games played and then rounding them to the nearest thousandth. Use a calculator or long division to check if the newspaper's numbers are accurate.

Dollar Wise

The most practical application of decimals is through the use of money. Use a few hypothetical situations such as the ones given here to give your child division practice as well as a better understanding of the value of a dollar.

- Choose a major purchase, such as a color TV, a new car, or a "boom box." Let your child find the purchase price in magazines or sale flyers. Have your child determine what it would cost each person if six friends decided to make the purchase, splitting the price equally.
- Choose a major purchase of interest to your child. Have your child divide the cost by the amount of weekly allowance to determine how many weeks he or she would need to save to make the purchase.

Science for Fifth Graders

You may find that at the fifth grade level, your child will be covering some of the same scientific topics covered at earlier grade levels. But fifth graders cover them in greater depth as their level of understanding and ability to grasp more abstract ideas is increasing.

The science curriculum is often divided into three major categories. Topics studied will vary by school or school district. Here are some science topics your child may encounter:

LIFE SCIENCE (PLANTS, ANIMALS, ECOLOGY)

- animal classifications—vertebrates or invertebrates; further classification of vertebrates into subgroups of mammals, birds, fish, reptiles, and amphibians
- plant life cycles
- ecosystems
- human body systems
- drug education

EARTH SCIENCE (EARTH, WEATHER, SPACE)

- Earth's structure
- changes in weather
- climate
- the solar system
- stars and constellations

PHYSICAL SCIENCE (MATTER, ENERGY)

- atoms and elements
- physical and chemical changes in matter
- motion and forces
- electricity
- energy resources

SCIENCE ACTIVITIES

Encourage your child to start collections related to any new interests.

Observe and Record

Provide a spiral notebook to help your child start a science journal. Take it along on a walk or a drive, even in the city. Encourage your child to record any interesting observations. Have your child note and sketch insects, other animals, or plants that catch his or her attention. Direct your child to include information such as where they were spotted, how many there were, what time of the day it was, and what they were doing. Invite your child to keep an ongoing list of questions that come up and to look for answers on TV, in books and magazines, at the library, or to find an expert to ask. This will make your child more aware of his or her environment.

Classification

Discuss with your child how items are grouped in the grocery store or discount store, then enlist his or her help in compiling the shopping list for your next store visit. Have your child group the items the way they would be grouped in the store. Explain that this will help you to shop more quickly without forgetting an item. It may take a bit longer, but it will give your child great practice with the scientific concept of categorizing and classifying.

Family Field Trips

Visits to museums, zoos, aquariums, botanical gardens, and planetariums can be great sources of information and will often spark new interests for your child. Tune in to any signs of interest and help your child to explore these areas further with library books, field guides, encyclopedias, reference books, or online resources if you have Internet access.

Collectible Collections

Children at this age are often fascinated by the idea of collecting. Collections are a great way for your child to learn firsthand about sorting and classifying. Encourage your child's choice whether it be coins, stamps, trading cards, books, action figures, rocks, seashells, or even buttons. Guide your child as needed in finding appropriate ways to display the collection. Scrapbooks, egg cartons, shoe boxes, or shelf space may be all it takes. If you have access to a computer, you can help your child catalog and file information about the collection as well.

SCIENTIFIC METHOD

A hands-on approach in the classroom most closely resembles the scientific method used by scientists. It involves exploration, trial and error, making hypotheses, and testing and changing hypotheses. It requires observation, keeping records, and comparing data. It results in discovery and learning. But even if your child's classroom uses a more traditional textbook approach to science, you can encourage these scientific methods at home by exploring, experimenting, experiencing, and discovering with your child.

Home Weather Station

Learning how to use household weather instruments such as thermometers, barometers, weather vanes, and rain gauges can help your child become more aware of weather patterns and changes. Suggest that your child record information from these instruments as well as personal observations about clouds and precipitation for several weeks, especially during a change of seasons when the weather changes are more pronounced.

Weather Maps

Encourage your child to make a scrapbook of weather maps found in the newspaper to go along with the recordings suggested above. Help your child to make inferences (educated guesses) about the observations and their relation to the information printed on the weather maps. Have your child make comparisons of the weekly outlook and the actual weather conditions.

Be a Weather Scout

Some weather stations have weather scouts who phone in more localized weather information. Employ your child as your personal weather scout and help him or her keep track of high and low temperatures and precipitation for your area. Suggest that your child try graphing the daily highs and lows for a week on one graph to make a comparison. He or she may also want to pick a city in another area of the country to watch and compare to your area.

Astronomy Fun

As parents, you may feel you cannot help your child learn about topics that you are not familiar with yourself. Try to remember that there is much benefit to be gained by exploring new worlds together with your child. He or she will gain factual information as well as the benefit of seeing your curiosity and interest in learning.

Begin an exploration of astronomy by learning about constellations. Pick out some exceptionally bright stars, distinct configurations of stars, or a familiar constellation like the Big Dipper. View the night skies several nights in a row and over the course of a few weeks or months. Try to find the same stars each night. Make note of changes in their appearance or location. Expensive telescopes are not necessary. If possible, view the night sky through binoculars. You will be surprised by how many more stars will appear. If you live in a large city, try driving out away from the bright city lights to see the difference in the night sky. If you live near a university or observatory that offers planetarium shows, visit a show with your child. Once your child's curiosity is peaked, find library books on astronomy and identify some of the constellations you've seen.

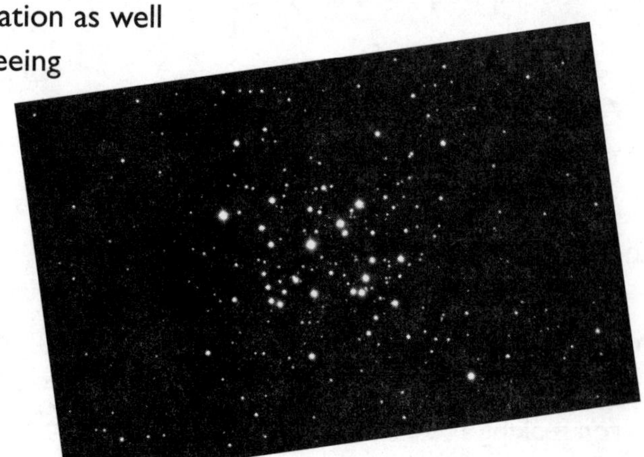

Garbage for the Garden?

Read the poem "Sarah Cynthia Sylvia Stout Would Not Take the Garbage Out" found in the book *Where The Sidewalk Ends* by Shel Silverstein (Harper & Row, 1974). Use it as a lead in to an environmental discussion on the importance of composting and recycling. Try and separate Sarah's collection of garbage into garbage that can be composted and garbage that cannot. (Plant products can be composted. Meat and dairy products cannot.) Add some rhyming recyclables to the list.

Carnivore-Omnivore-Herbivore

Play a variation of the game Rock, Paper, Scissors. In this animal kingdom version, each player secretly jots down an animal name. Then all players display their names. To determine who wins, players must first say whether their animal is a carnivore, omnivore, or herbivore. In this version, a carnivore beats an omnivore, an omnivore beats a herbivore, and a herbivore beats a carnivore following the logic of a food chain in which a carnivore would eat an omnivore, an omnivore might eat a herbivore, and a herbivore feeds on the plants nourished by all decaying matter including carnivores.

Animal Puzzles

Players challenge each other by giving their opponent the name of an animal. For each letter in the animal's name, the opponent must think of some characteristic of that animal or its habitat, a common behavior, or a predator or prey of that animal. Award one point for each answer a player comes up with.

Butting battles
cl**I**ffs
char**G**e
Herds
b**O**bcats
Rocky Mountains
hor**N**s

Field Guides

Children at this age often enjoy browsing through field guides. They are available on a wide range of topics, such as plants, birds, trees, flowers, insects, seashells, and more. Even those written at a more advanced level can be fascinating and beneficial because of the detailed, colorful drawings. The *Peterson Field Guides* and the *Golden Guides* are two series readily available at libraries, bookstores, and even museum gift shops.

Super Software Tip

If you have a computer with a CD-ROM drive, consider purchasing CyberCraft's *Fun With Electronics*. This program comes with a hands-on electronic workbench. Children follow the step-by-step directions on the computer to assemble circuit projects, such as a burglar alarm.

Social Studies for Fifth Graders

Social Studies in today's elementary classroom is more than a history class. It draws on many different disciplines, such as anthropology, archaeology, economics, geography, political science, and sociology to name just a few.

Even though there is a specific content taught at any given grade level, memorization of facts and information is not the main focus. The emphasis is on the acquisition of skills necessary for understanding and interpreting the information. Map skills are emphasized, as well as the skills needed for interpreting and creating tables, diagrams, charts, graphs, and timelines. Developing critical thinking skills is valued more than rote memorization. At the simplest level this would involve naming, listing and describing, but more important are the abilities to apply information to new situations, make comparisons, identify main issues, form generalizations, make predictions, and draw conclusions. The emphasis is on helping students think for themselves.

At the fifth grade level these skills are presented in the context of the history and heritage of the United States. Some of the areas covered include these:

* the Native American groups prior to the Europeans' arrival
* early explorers and discoverers
* the New England, Middle, and Southern colonies
* the Revolutionary War
* the Constitution and the United States government
* slavery and the Civil War
* westward expansion
* the Industrial Revolution
* World War I and World War II
* the Great Depression
* current events

Finally, it is the goal of the Social Studies curriculum to help students develop an ability for responsible decision making and good citizenship in their community—local, national, and global.

MAP ACTIVITIES

Map Happy

Map skills are important at all grade levels and any reinforcement of these skills will help your child to be more successful in social studies. Take advantage of map reading opportunities in your daily life. If you run across a map while at the mall, spend a few minutes looking it over with your child. Find where you are, where you've been, or some of your favorite stores. Watch for maps of amusement parks, museums, zoos, and campgrounds that you visit. These are often included in their brochures. Encourage your child to use them to help plan your visit.

Local Maps

Look for maps of your community. Telephone books often include a city or regional map. State maps are readily available at gas stations and are sometimes distributed free by politicians. Use the maps for these activities:

- Involve your child in finding your usual route to familiar places and to friends' and relatives' homes. Help your child map an alternate route to some of these places. Try using it the next time one of those places is your destination.
- Compare two routes on the map. Estimate the distances and predict which is shorter. Clock the two routes to check your estimates and predictions.
- Get lost! Randomly select a spot on a city, county, or state map and challenge your child to find the way from that point back home.

Not For Computers Only

The *Carmen Sandiego* series developed by Brøderbund is a fun way to explore geography. The series includes computer software, board games, and TV programs relating to world geography, U.S. geography, and history.

Draw It!

Challenge family members to draw and label from memory a map of your state, the country, North America, or the world. Then gather any maps or globes you have. Compare your masterpieces with the professionals'. Repeat the activity letting family members use the maps as a guide.

How Far?

Find a map that includes a scale; it can be a state map, country map, or world map. Each of you choose a city. Look at the scale and have each person write an estimate for the actual distance between the two cities. Help your child measure the length between the two points on the map and use the scale to calculate the distance. Whose estimate was closer?

Is It North of San Francisco?

Play this game to practice direction words. Use a map of your state, another state, or a country. One player chooses a city. The other players look at the map and try to guess the city by asking questions that can be answered yes or no. All questions must contain a direction word, such as *west* or *northeast*.

Sports Geography

If your child is interested in sports, cash in on that interest. Help your child locate the hometowns of his or her favorite teams in one or more sports. Have your child cut small flags out of construction paper and write the names of the teams on them. Attach an old U.S. map to a bulletin board and tack the team flags to the correct location. Suggest that your child color code the flags by sport.

A Newsworthy State

Armed with a highlighting marker, a ruler, and a newspaper, you and your child can do some serious detective work. Using the ruler (or a piece of cardboard) to help with skimming the fine newspaper print, search the paper for mention of any of the 50 states. When you find a state, highlight it or jot it down on a piece of paper. See how many you can discover in one day's paper. Try this activity several different days and compare your results.

What a Trip!

Where would your child like to go on vacation? Yellowstone Park? Disney World? Washington, D.C.? Maui? All of these places? Invite family members to each plan a dream vacation that lasts one month. Compare plans and dreams.

Map Madness

Many of the cities that can be found around the country go by very unusual and interesting names. Work with your child to find some of these unusual names on a state or U.S. map. Suggest a category and see how many names you and your child can find that fit the category. Some possible categories are color names, weather words, plant names, famous people, animals, girls' names, or boys' names.

Facts About the Fifty States

Your child can use the fact sheet on the next page for reference or for these activities:

- **Cover the state column and try to name each state by reading its postal abbreviation or capital.**
- **Number and list the states in the order they entered the Union.**
- **Draw illustrations to match state nicknames. guessing each**

Fill in the Map

Page 87 contains a blank U.S. map. You may want to make several copies of it so your child can use it in more than one way. Ideas:

- **Fill in the names, capital cities, or postal abbreviations of each state.**
- **Draw mountain ranges and major rivers.**
- **Color code the map to show the original colonies separated by regions—New England, Middle, Southern.**
- **Color code the map to show Union and Confederate states and territories during the Civil War.**
- **Number the states from 1 to 50 in the order they entered the Union.**

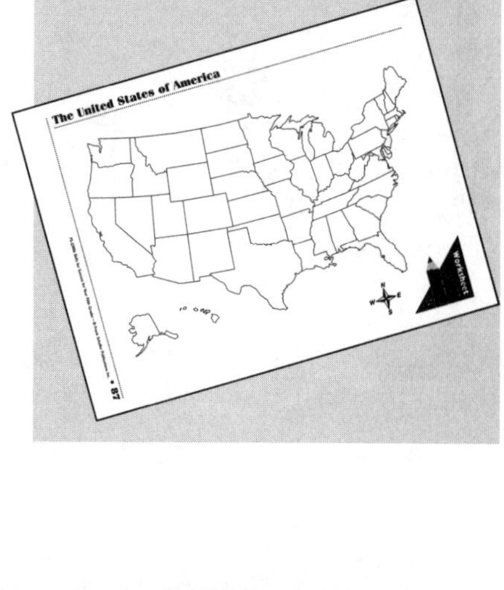

★ ★ ★ ★ OUR 50 STATES FACT SHEET ★ ★ ★ ★

State	Capital	Abbreviation	Nickname	Date Entered Union
Alabama	Montgomery	AL	Heart of Dixie	December 14, 1819
Alaska	Juneau	AK	Last Frontier	January 3, 1959
Arizona	Phoenix	AZ	Grand Canyon State	February 14, 1912
Arkansas	Little Rock	AR	Land of Opportunity	June 15, 1836
California	Sacramento	CA	Golden State	September 9, 1850
Colorado	Denver	CO	Centennial State	August 1, 1876
Connecticut	Hartford	CT	Constitution State	January 9, 1788
Delaware	Dover	DE	First State	December 7, 1787
Florida	Tallahassee	FL	Sunshine State	March 3, 1845
Georgia	Atlanta	GA	Empire State of the South	January 2, 1788
Hawaii	Honolulu	HI	Aloha State	August 21, 1959
Idaho	Boise	ID	Gem State	July 3, 1890
Illinois	Springfield	IL	Land of Lincoln	December 3, 1818
Indiana	Indianapolis	IN	Hoosier State	December 11, 1816
Iowa	Des Moines	IA	Hawkeye State	December 28, 1846
Kansas	Topeka	KS	Sunflower State	January 29, 1861
Kentucky	Frankfort	KY	Bluegrass State	June 1, 1792
Louisiana	Baton Rouge	LA	Pelican State	April 30, 1812
Maine	Augusta	ME	Pine Tree State	March 15, 1820
Maryland	Annapolis	MD	Old Line State	April 28, 1788
Massachusetts	Boston	MA	Bay State	February 6, 1788
Michigan	Lansing	MI	Wolverine State	January 26, 1837
Minnesota	St. Paul	MN	Gopher State	May 11, 1858
Mississippi	Jackson	MS	Magnolia State	December 10, 1817
Missouri	Jefferson City	MO	Show Me State	August 10, 1821
Montana	Helena	MT	Treasure State	November 8, 1889
Nebraska	Lincoln	NE	Cornhusker State	March 1, 1867
Nevada	Carson City	NV	Silver State	October 31, 1864
New Hampshire	Concord	NH	Granite State	June 21, 1788
New Jersey	Trenton	NJ	Garden State	December 18, 1787
New Mexico	Santa Fe	NM	Land of Enchantment	January 6, 1912
New York	Albany	NY	Empire State	July 26, 1788
North Carolina	Raleigh	NC	Tar Heel State	November 21, 1789
North Dakota	Bismarck	ND	Flickertail State	November 2, 1889
Ohio	Columbus	OH	Buckeye State	March 1, 1803
Oklahoma	Oklahoma City	OK	Sooner State	November 16, 1907
Oregon	Salem	OR	Beaver State	February 14, 1859
Pennsylvania	Harrisburg	PA	Keystone State	December 12, 1787
Rhode Island	Providence	RI	Ocean State	May 29, 1790
South Carolina	Columbia	SC	Palmetto State	May 23, 1788
South Dakota	Pierre	SD	Mount Rushmore State	November 2, 1889
Tennessee	Nashville	TN	Volunteer State	June 1, 1796
Texas	Austin	TX	Lone Star State	December 29, 1845
Utah	Salt Lake City	UT	Beehive State	January 4, 1896
Vermont	Montpelier	VT	Green Mountain State	March 4, 1791
Virginia	Richmond	VA	Mother of Presidents	June 25, 1788
Washington	Olympia	WA	Evergreen State	November 11, 1889
West Virginia	Charleston	WV	Mountain State	June 20, 1863
Wisconsin	Madison	WI	Badger State	May 29, 1848
Wyoming	Cheyenne	WY	Equality State	July 10, 1890

HISTORY ACTIVITIES

Historical Fiction and Biographies

Children's literature is an interesting resource for learning about the past.

- For light fare, your child may enjoy reading about Ben Franklin or Paul Revere from the viewpoints of a mouse and a horse in these books by Robert Lawson:
  Ben and Me
  Mr. Revere and I
- Jean Fritz has written several biographies that help to bring history alive for children. Here are some of her titles:
  The Double Life of Pocahontas
  Will You Sign Here, John Hancock?
  You Want Women to Vote, Lizzie Stanton?
- The *Little House* series by Laura Ingalls Wilder presents many fascinating details of frontier life.
- Mildred D. Taylor's award-winning novels describe life for an African-American family in Mississippi in the early 1900s:
  Roll of Thunder, Hear My Cry
  The Well: David's Story
- The *American Girls* series covers five different periods—colonial, pioneer, Civil War, turn-of-the-20th century, and World War II—through the adventures and everyday life of a young girl living during that period.
- These authors are well-known for their historical fiction: Clyde Bulla, Scott O'Dell, Elizabeth Speare, Yoshiko Uchida, and Laurence Yep.

Picture Perfect Past

Share old photographs and artifacts (old dishes, tools, jewelry, toys, books) that you may have with your child. If you don't have any personal items of this type, browse through a few antique stores with your child. Chances are you will find some very willing teachers in the proprietors of these stores.

Learning from the Past

Grandparents, elderly neighbors, and friends can be valuable sources of information about the past. Encourage your child to do informal interviews with these people. Guide your child in thinking of some specific areas to focus the discussions. Narrow topics down to simple daily activities like how they cooked their food, washed their clothes, traveled to school, or dressed for school. What kinds of school supplies did they need? What kind of rules did they have to follow? Hobbies or games they had when young would also be interesting. Your child might find it fascinating to make an audio tape or videotape of the interviews.

Local Resources

Take advantage of any history museums, sites, restorations, or re-enactments available locally to help bring different periods of history to life for your child. These can provide excellent opportunities for family outings, broaden your child's interests, and lead very naturally to "follow-up" reading and the desire to learn more. They will also add richly to your child's base of experience which in turn will lead to better comprehension of content area reading.

SOCIAL STUDIES ACTIVITIES

Social Studies in a Flash

Continue to reinforce what your child has learned about different important people, places, and events by creating a set of flash cards. Together with your child write the name of a person, place, or event on one side of a 3" x 5" index card. On the back jot a few notes or phrases to remind you of important facts or related information about the subject. Continue to add to your deck throughout the school year. To use the cards, show one card at a time to your child. If your child can tell you something about the word on the card, he or she wins that card. After earning a set number of cards, such as five, your child earns the right to flash the cards to you. He or she will delight in this opportunity to try and stump you! It is not necessary to remember and give all the information on the card. By repeated use of the cards, your child will gradually arrive at a broader understanding of each subject.

Famous Words

Citizenship involves knowing about your country's symbols and important documents. Use page 88 to check or supplement your child's knowledge.

Active Citizenship

Stress to your child that tasks both large and small can bring about positive results. Some suggestions might include picking up litter, helping with recycling, visiting a nursing home, donating toys and clothes to a charitable organization, helping an elderly or disabled neighbor with household chores, helping to maintain a local park, or serving in some way at a church or school fundraiser. Following your lead in any of these activities will make the biggest impression on your child.

A Timely Timeline

Help your child keep track of the many people, places, and events he or she learns about by making an ongoing timeline.

The responsibility and importance of good citizenship can become more meaningful for your child at this age if you help him or her find appropriate ways to volunteer in the community.

As new material is covered in class, your child can come home and add it to his or her personal timeline. Start with a long roll of paper. Fax paper or continuous-feed computer paper would work well. If none is available to you, you could cut inexpensive wrapping paper into about 10-inch-wide strips. Tape several strips together. Or tape sheets of typing paper together, adding new sheets for each period of study. Help your child to measure and mark off the years at equal intervals. It is not necessary to label every year. Every 5 to 10 years is fine. Display the timeline throughout the year on a bedroom or family room wall or tape one end to an empty paper towel roll and roll the timeline up like a scroll. Unroll it to add new information. Your child may enjoy illustrating some of the people or events along the timeline as well.

Art for Fifth Graders

At the fifth grade level, children are developing increased observation skills and are paying greater attention to detail. They are generally concerned that their end results look realistic, or life-like. Their ability to describe, interpret, evaluate, compare, and respond to their own work and the work of others is growing.

The art curriculum at this level will strive to reinforce previous artistic learning experiences while challenging students to expand their abilities. As with other curriculum areas, the specific content may vary by school or school district.

Although many of the mediums and processes mentioned in the box to the right may have been used previously to produce end products, at this level the projects will be more advanced and complicated, challenging the students' use of artistic techniques.

- **They will be exposed to drawing using mediums such as pen and ink, charcoal, and scratch boards with greater attention to detail. They will continue to work with contour and gesture drawing techniques.**
- **They will employ various painting techniques with tempera and watercolors.**
- **They will attempt more advanced printing methods.**
- **They will create free standing or hanging sculptures.**
- **They will understand the characteristics of clay and the techniques for joining clay. They will use their knowledge to produce a piece of pottery.**
- **They will combine various elements and principles of design within their works, including pattern, texture, line, color, space, and balance.**
- **Because of their increased abilities to analyze and compare, attention will be given to art from other cultures and periods in history as well from different artists and different art styles.**

ART ACTIVITIES

Supply the Supplies

Provide your child with a variety of art supplies and materials at home. They do not need to be expensive. Scraps of fabric and wood, odds and ends like spools and buttons, recycled items like egg cartons, margarine containers, and cardboard tubes, and a few basic supplies like glue, paint, brushes, tape, markers, colored pencils, and paper will allow your child to experiment and create. You can find suggestions for simple projects in many resources—children's craft books, children's magazines like *Crayola Kids, Highlights for Children*, and *Pack-O-Fun*, and the family magazine *Family Fun*. This exposure will help children enjoy and feel comfortable with art, just as the presence of books in the home can help them to be better readers. Even though children at this age do enjoy craft kits, this less-structured approach will encourage greater possibilities for exploration and creativity.

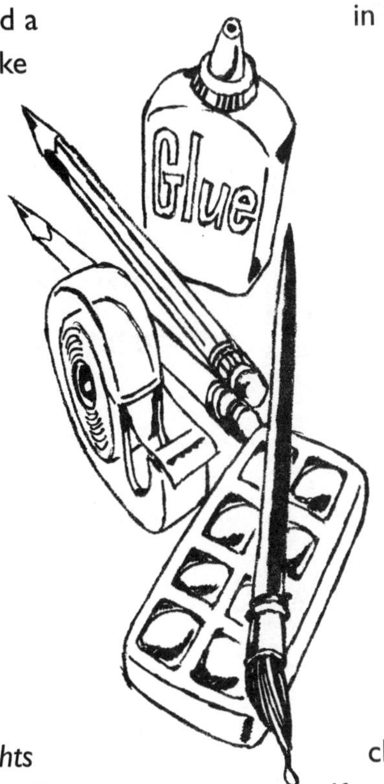

Art Museums

A visit to an art museum may rank right up there with a trip to the dentist in the mind of your child. If this is so, try a new approach. Before your next visit, make a list of things to look for in the paintings. Get your child involved in compiling the list. Include things like a sunny day, a dog (or another favorite animal), a boat, a monster, a favorite food. Then treat your visit like a scavenger hunt and see how many of the items you can check off your list. If you don't have access to an art museum, find a volume of art works at the library and try the same activity.

Art Detective

You can encourage an appreciation for art in your young art connoisseur by playing art detective. Choose a print in an art book or on a poster and together study the print for a set amount of time or about 10 minutes. Then cover the print and each try to list as many details as you can remember from the print, again allow a set amount of time. When the time is up, compare your lists to the print. Try to find details that you both missed. This will really get your child to look closely.

One technique used to appreciate a piece of artwork is to study it for an extended length of time and really get to know the work.

The Children's Section

Often art museums and arts and crafts exhibits offer a children's area, providing projects and the necessary materials to complete them as well as experienced craftspeople to assist. Take the time to allow your child to participate. The craftspeople can provide the ideas and expertise that you may feel you lack in this area.

MORE ART ACTIVITIES

Involve your child in the design and creation of invitations and cards for special family events and holidays.

An Invitation to Art

When creating invitations and cards, encourage your child to try different techniques using rubber stamps, calligraphy pens, potato prints, stickers, glitter, fabric paints, and collages of magazine photos.

No Joke

Children at this age are fascinated with riddles and jokes, often seeming to have their own unique humor. Encourage your child to express himself or herself artistically while illustrating a handmade booklet of favorite riddles or jokes. Present it to grandparents as a special gift.

Share a Hobby

As adults, many of us have learned to enrich our lives with hobbies involving artistic expression. Encourage your child to join you in your own interest, whether it is ceramics, photography, quilting, woodworking, jewelry making, cake decorating, gardening, or something else. Help develop lifelong, stress-relieving interests that your child will appreciate for years to come while he or she is also developing an interest in art itself.

Frame It

Give your child the sense that you value his or her artwork. Find ways to display it and show it off. Find some wall space along a stairway or hallway for this purpose. Purchase a few inexpensive frames in which to display the work. Change the pictures in the frames periodically. Large, inexpensive bulletin boards also work well for this purpose.

"Play It Again"

The time devoted to art in the school system is often very limited and provides little time for your child to explore a method or medium as much as he or she may like. If your child seems to have especially enjoyed a particular project or process, help supply the necessary materials at home so he or she can experiment with it further.

Children's Illustrators

Peruse through the picture book section of the library. Invite your child to gather and compare several books from different illustrators to get a feel for their style. You could also choose the same folktale, such as *Red Riding Hood*, and see how different artists express it. Your child may want to mimic the style of a favorite illustrator to create pictures for a story he or she has written. Here are some acclaimed illustrators whose works you may want to begin with: Jan Brett, Tomie dePaola, Leo and Diane Dillon, Trina Schart Hyman, Brian Pinkney, Jerry Pinkney, Janet Stevens, Chris Van Allsburg, Vera B. Williams, and Ed Young.

Music for Fifth Graders

The goal of music education at the fifth grade level is to continue to develop your child's music literacy and appreciation for music. Through the music program your child will recognize the emotional and creative outlet that music offers and realize its potential as a life-long source of enjoyment and relaxation.

Through further study of written music, your child will gain extended knowledge of musical notation.

Fifth graders often study scales, rhythm, meter, notes and note values, word symbols, rests, and other signs. They learn to identify notes on the staff.

Through experience in singing and performing, your child will learn more about tonality, voice control, articulation, expression, and two- and three-part harmony.

Fifth graders should be able to verbalize their knowledge of music through the proper use of specialized music vocabulary.

The fifth grader will be given various listening experiences to help differentiate between major and minor sounds, to recognize different instruments of the orchestra, and to experience different types of music.

Fifth graders may also get first hand experience on select instruments such as the recorder, suitable for group instruction.

Your child's musical experience at this level may overlap other fine arts to include exposure to movement and dance.

It is hoped that fifth graders will gain an awareness of the profound effect of music on their daily lives and the potential for music in their future, whether it be in their careers or personal time.

Instrumental Music

In many schools, fifth grade is the year children are able to begin instrumental music, or band as it is commonly called. If the opportunity exists at your school, encourage your child to participate. You may want your child to take private lessons as an alternative or in addition to band. Studying an instrument provides many benefits besides the obvious one of creating music—it teaches discipline, commitment, and in the case of band, teamwork.

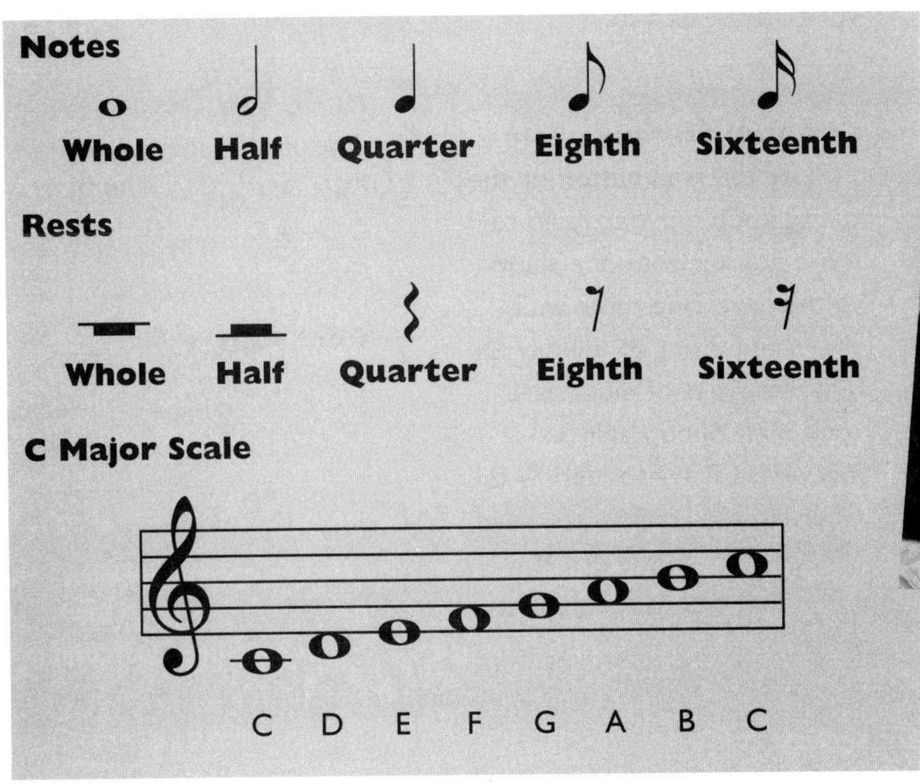

MUSIC ACTIVITIES

Music All Around Us

Call your child's attention to the numerous places that he or she hears music besides on the radio. After pointing out a few examples, encourage your child to make a list of all the times and places that he or she encounters music throughout the day. The list may include TV programs, cartoons, stores, on-hold on the telephone, elevators, and doctors' and dentists' offices. See if your child can classify the music as happy, sad, exciting, relaxing, and so on. Discuss what these situations would be like without the music.

Mystery Sounds

Arm your child with a tape recorder and a blank tape and give your child the assignment of recording some mystery sounds or noises in his or her environment. Suggest that your child also include some theme songs from favorite cartoons and TV shows. Next, encourage your child to play the tape for friends and family members, testing how many sounds and themes each person can correctly identify.

Exposure is Excellent

Try to expose your child to a variety of types of music through the use of the radio and tapes or CDs borrowed from the public library. Be willing to listen to the music your child likes also.

Channel Surfing

Use the scan button or the tuning knob on your radio to move quickly from one station to the next. Take turns with your child trying to identify the different types of music: jazz, rock, rap, country, spiritual, folk, classical. Try to identify the different instruments you hear at each stop on the dial. Play name that tune or name that artist.

Whistle While You Work

Brighten up your chores with music. Use different types and tempos to help set the pace or inspire the forces.

Live or on Tape

Attend live concerts and productions if possible. If not, rent videos of musicals showing different styles of music and dance. Or check out tapes or CD recordings of the music. Here are several titles your child may enjoy:

Videos and Recordings

The Sound of Music
Fiddler on the Roof
The Wizard of Oz
West Side Story
The King and I
My Fair Lady
Oklahoma
Peter Pan
Camelot
Grease

Recordings

The Phantom of the Opera
Les Misérables
Cats

Physical Education for Fifth Graders

Your fifth grade child will learn more from physical education class than the individual skills associated with a variety of popular sports. It will also be a time when he or she will learn to appreciate the qualities of good sportsmanship, fair play, and team effort. Your child will learn that physical activity is a vital part of a healthful lifestyle and will hopefully develop some lifelong interests of a physical nature. Of course these values and concepts will be developed through involvement in a variety of physical activities and sports. To the children, the sports and other activities may seem like an end in themselves. In the physical education curriculum, they are the means for developing various movement and coordination skills.

Their physical education program will hopefully help them realize the enjoyment, positive feelings, and relationships with others that can result from participation in physical activity.

At a fifth grade level, students should:

- **learn to support, lift, and control weight from feet to hands, at slow and fast speeds in the context of activities such as gymnastics, tumbling, and fitness exercises**
- **be able to hand dribble and foot dribble a ball and maintain control of it in game situations**
- **learn to strike a ball with controlled direction using a variety of implements and body parts in games such as baseball and volleyball**
- **develop patterns and combinations of movements and be able to repeat sequences of taught movements through experiences with line dances, square dances, aerobics, and jumping rope**

- **learn to throw, catch, and kick properly in game situations**
- **assess their physical fitness and strive to achieve appropriate levels**
- **learn rules and strategies for selected physical activities**
- **learn to take responsibility for their own safety and the safety of others while engaged in physical activities**

Children Learn What They Live

As parents, your example speaks louder than words in this area as in so many other areas. If your child sees you regularly engaged in physical activity, he or she will be more likely to choose physical activities, too. You can encourage your child even more by including him or her in the activities that you enjoy. You may have to change your pace for awhile to accommodate your child, but maybe he or she will reciprocate in a few years and slow down for you! If you are not active enough yourself, now would be a good time to try a new hobby.

Activity Log

Have your child keep a log of personal activities for several days or weeks to determine just how active he or she really is. Each entry should include information such as the date, type of activity, and amount of time spent on the activity. Your child may also want to classify each as active or passive. It might be even more encouraging for your child (and healthy for you) if you do likewise. Together you and your child can take steps to achieve a more even balance between time spent on passive and active activities.

Tone It Down

As children develop new skills, you want it to be a positive experience, making them feel good about themselves. If you are willing to modify the rules and equipment, your child can gain competence at the sport while enjoying the process. As mentioned previously, this may mean slowing down the pace. In some games, it might help to use a smaller or lighter ball, a smaller playing area, or lower nets and hoops.

Bountiful Balls

Not all balls are created equal. Choosing the right ball can make all the difference when learning to catch. Make a variety of balls available to your child. Koosh™ balls (they appear to be made from several broken rubberbands) are especially good for beginners. Their weight makes them easy to throw far and their texture makes them easy to catch. Nerf™ balls take away a lot of the fear associated with catching because they are soft and don't hurt. Scaled down versions of basketballs and footballs are easier for small hands to handle skillfully.

How Far? How Long? How Fast?

Hold family fitness fests where you see how far each person can throw a ball, how long he or she can hang above a bar, or how fast each person can run an obstacle course. Sneak in some math practice by involving your child in measuring distances or times. Have each family member do an activity two or more times so it's a competition against yourself, trying to beat your personal best.

Hiking, biking, swimming, skating, bowling, canoeing, and tennis, to name just a few, all make good family activities.

BEST FRIENDS

Just about everyone, except for the occasional loner, longs to find that perfect soulmate, that kindred spirit, that one person that will truly understand and with whom we can share our hopes and dreams. The problem is that at this age most children are still searching and are anxious to apply this title to each new person that they begin to grow close to. Encourage your child to be open to making many new friends. If your daughter (or son) meets someone who wants to have an exclusive friendship, suggest that your child come right out and tell the friend that she is glad to have her as a friend, but that she still wants to meet and associate with others. If a "best friend" seems to be cutting your son (or daughter) out in favor of a new "best friend," your child may want to tell his friend that he is glad that he is making new friends, but that he still wants to remain friends also. Help your child realize that even best friends don't have to do everything together.

IF YOUR CHILD DOESN'T FEEL LIKE PART OF THE GROUP

Often at this age, groups or cliques will begin to form. Being left out will make your child feel like he or she is different or odd. Realize that most cliques have one strong leader and everyone else feels more or less a part of the group depending on the particular day. Encourage your child to try to make friends with individuals rather than attempt to fit into a group. Help your child decide what is important to him or her and to avoid compromising beliefs just to be accepted. To avoid trouble, your child should resist the urge to join in on talking about others behind their backs. It generally backfires.

IF YOUR CHILD IS A LEADER

Whether your child is a leader or a follower depends mainly on his or her personality. Either one is OK, but the child who is a leader will need to recognize that there is a certain amount of responsibility that goes along with it. It may feel good to be at the center of attention, but others will follow his or her lead whether it is a good example or a bad example.

IF YOUR CHILD IS A FOLLOWER

Not all children have the type of personality needed to be a leader. In fact, many people are very content to be followers. This is perfectly all right. What followers need to realize is that they must choose who they will follow very carefully. Never just follow blindly.

RULES

In every school and classroom you are bound to find a set of rules for the children to follow. In most cases there will also be a set of consequences that the children can expect should they deviate from these rules. These expectations and consequences are established in order to maintain a climate in which effective learning may take place. The rules generally spell out how the students should treat the people and property around them. They deal with attitudes and behaviors that are appropriate for a school setting. Oftentimes rules focus on asking students to use good manners when dealing with others. Since there is not always agreement about what is considered acceptable behavior, a written set of rules and consequences is very helpful in letting children and parents know exactly what is expected of them.

Conflicting Rules

At some point your child may encounter a school or class rule that differs from your home rules. Your child should never be expected to follow any rule that he or she feels is unsafe or morally wrong. If this should occur, let your child know that it is alright to disagree with the teacher as long as he or she does it at an appropriate time and in a polite and respectful way. Assure your child that he or she can count on you to act as an advocate on your child's behalf should such a situation arise.

Some Typical Rules

Whatever the rules, they will usually fall into several categories: respect and consideration for others, wise use of time and materials, and safety. Read through these rules with your child. Think of other examples for each category listed.

Respect and Consideration for Others

- raise your hand to speak
- do not interrupt
- do not disturb others who are studying
- follow directions
- no swearing
- do not damage the property of others
- no stealing
- no cheating
- no back talk

Safety

- walk in an orderly fashion
- keep hands, feet, and other objects to yourself
- do not leave the school grounds without permission

Wise Use of Time and Materials

- be prepared for class
- be on time for class
- take proper care of supplies

PROBLEM SOLVING

At this age, as at every age, your child will face some very typical problems and maybe some that are not quite as typical. Whatever problems arise for your child, it is important to remember that each problem he or she encounters is new to him or her. Your child's confusion and inexperience with how to handle it is what makes it a problem. This can be both frustrating and frightening to your child. You may have the urge to jump in with advice and help, but your child no longer wants as much supervision or intervention and will increasingly need to rely on his or her own problem-solving strategies.

As parents, we hope that our children will be prepared to handle the problems that they will undoubtedly face.

Some Typical Problems

The majority of the problems that will arise for your child will fall into one of several categories. They may be problems with other children, problems with teachers, organizational problems, or problems with more personal issues. The following pages give examples of these problems and some suggestions that may help.

General Tips

Encourage your child to be respectful and polite and to choose an appropriate time to discuss problems with others to get the best results.

Help your child identify the chain of command that applies to him or her and to use it to get results. This may mean first dealing directly with friends or teachers, then moving on to parents, principals, or other persons in authority. Assure your child of your support if needed.

Encourage your child to talk about little problems before they become big ones.

Explain to your child how speaking loudly, clearly, and directly usually yields the best results.

Help your child brainstorm all possible solutions to a problem and to look at the problems from a different point of view—the other child's, the teacher's, and so on. Try to work backwards by identifying the desired outcome and then deciding how that outcome can be reached.

Avoid being openly critical of your child's teacher, texts, school, or assignments in your efforts to work through problems with them.

Avoid overscheduling. Sometimes more rest or sleep can make all the difference.

If your child becomes frustrated with a problem, have him or her take a break and come back to it later, but stick to it. Generally problems don't just go away by themselves.

PROBLEMS WITH OTHER KIDS

If Your Child Is Being Picked On

Sometimes the simplest solution is the best. Your child should just walk away if he or she can. This, of course, isn't always possible. As a second option, your child shouldn't be afraid to speak up for himself or herself. Something as simple as "I don't like that. Quit it." may be all it takes. Your child should avoid getting into a lengthy argument, but should speak in a voice as loud, clear, and assertive as he or she can muster. If this does not work, your child may need to seek adult intervention. If there is danger of physical harm, he or she should seek adult help immediately.

Bragging

Children may brag to get attention or because they feel insecure with themselves. Help your child to realize that the kind of attention that bragging gets is not positive attention and that it will tend to push people away which is the exact opposite response that he or she is seeking. At this age your child may have some difficulty distinguishing between bragging and sharing enthusiasm and pride in an activity or accomplishment. Let your child know that it is good to feel proud of what he or she has done and to share it with others, as long as your child doesn't come across sounding like his or her accomplishments are always the biggest and the best.

Picking Teams

When children pick teams for sports, it can be a painful experience. Those that are picked first are invariably the ones with the most skill or the ones that are most popular. It's an age–old problem and there isn't much that we as adults can do to intervene. At best, encourage your child to keep playing. Only by playing can he or she hope to improve. Offer to practice some of the skills with your child at home to help him or her become a more valuable player. Try to convince your child not to let this experience ruin the game for him or her.

Good advice at this age is to stay away from trouble in order to avoid guilt by association, even if your child chooses not to tell.

Tattling

Children usually no longer tattle at this age largely because of peer pressure. The problem at this age is getting them to understand that there are situations that should be reported to an adult. If someone your child knows is involved in something that could be harmful to that person or to someone else, your child should indeed tell.

When the Whole Class Is Punished

This is bound to happen at some point in your child's school career. It is generally discouraged, but it happens. It continues to happen to all of us, even as adults. Many suffer the consequences for the actions of a few. A few people shoplift. We all pay higher prices. A few vandalize a park. The park is closed to all. It isn't fair of course, but it does happen. Sometimes the teacher just does not have the time or the means to determine who the guilty individuals are. By punishing the whole, maybe the teacher is hoping to bring peer pressure to play against the real culprits. Suggest to your child that he or she just bear with it and look at it as punishment for something he did wrong that he didn't get caught for. If it happens continually, you may want to discuss it with your child's principal who may in turn be able to offer the teacher some guidance in other means of dealing with problems.

Ability Groups

When ability grouping is used, the students generally know who is in the "high group" and who is in the "low group" even if the teacher is careful not to designate them as such. Your child may feel that the activities of the other group look like more fun, or he or she may want to be in the same group with buddies. Either way, try to help your child understand that by being in the group that matches his or her skills, your child will have a greater chance to succeed.

If Your Child Doesn't Understand Something

Learning to speak up and ask questions is the best solution here. If your child isn't sure what question to ask, he or she should just ask the teacher to repeat the explanation. Your child may be afraid that by asking questions he or she might sound dumb. Other students will probably be grateful that someone had the guts to speak up.

Assure your child that if he or she doesn't understand, there are bound to be others who don't understand and who are also afraid to speak up.

ORGANIZATIONAL PROBLEMS

Your Child Forgets Homework

This can be a frightening situation in a class with a strict late assignment policy. It is best if your child informs the teacher as soon as possible. If it's a critical assignment, you may want to bring it. Your child may be given the opportunity to redo it during free time or to bring it in a day late, maybe with a parent's signature to verify that it was done on time. In some cases your child may be expected to suffer the consequences of an incomplete assignment. It may seem harsh to see your child penalized, but it is best to support your child's teacher. Realize that the teacher also has your child's best interests at heart and is trying to help him or her develop personal responsibility. Point out to your child that even adults must often suffer the consequences of "forgetting." How often do you suppose police officers hear the excuse, "I just forgot to use my turn signal . . . to slow down in that school zone . . ." and still hand out a ticket?

Your Child Forgets Lunch

Find out in advance what the school's policy is on this matter. Your child may be able to call you to drop it off. If this is not possible because of work or lack of transportation, he or she may be able to eat hot lunch on credit and pay later. You may want to have your child hide an extra dollar or two in his or her backpack to have on hand in case he or she forgets lunch or lunch money. Whatever the policy or situation, it is unlikely that a school will let a child go hungry.

Not Enough Time to Complete Work

In this situation you may first want to determine if the incomplete work is due to dawdling. Encourage your child to ask for extra time if he or she needs it. If this is a continual problem you will probably want to discuss it with your child's teacher to determine the reason for it and to plan an appropriate course of action, whether that be extra help, steps to eliminate daydreaming, or testing to determine a learning disability.

If Being Forgetful Is a Pattern

If forgetting homework or lunch is a common occurrence, have your child prepare those items and place them in the backpack the night before. Avoid hectic, stressful mornings. The fewer the items that need to be done in the morning, the greater the chances that nothing will be forgotten.

Your Child Doesn't Feel Well

Fifth graders should realize that if they are nauseous, they are not expected to raise their hands and wait for permission to go to the restroom. Most children in their school career have at least one day when they become sick and need to be picked up early. If you are not available to pick up your child, a friend or neighbor that you have listed on the school's emergency health card may be called. Be sure your child knows what arrangements you have made so that he or she is not doubly upset.

Problems at Home

Abuse, alcoholism, divorce, absence of a loved one, serious illness of a family member, or parent's loss of job are all serious situations that could severely trouble your child. At this age he or she is old enough to realize what is going on, but maybe not fully understand it. Never try to ignore the problems and pretend that your child might not notice. If you feel unable to talk to your child about these or any serious issues, seek help from a family counselor or a support person at your child's school, such as a guidance counselor or school psychologist.

You Are Not Alone

Sometimes children feel they are the only one with a problem and are afraid to talk to others about it. Or they may have a friend who is going through a difficult time and not understand why that friend is being unusually quiet or loud, shy or bossy, sad or angry. If you are aware of your child's concerns, you may want to guide him or her to one of these or other books to see how children in similar situations feel and act.

How It Feels to Live With a Physical Disability by Jill Krementz (Simon & Schuster, 1992) [Other titles in this series include *How It Feels to Fight for Your Life*, *How It Feels When a Parent Dies*, and *How It Feels When Parents Divorce*]

It's Perfectly Normal: Changing Bodies, Growing Up, Sex & Sexual Health by Robie H. Harris (Candlewick, 1994)

Talking About Stepfamilies by Maxine B. Rosenberg (Bradbury, 1990) [Other titles by this author include *Not My Family: Sharing the Truth About Alcoholism* and *Growing Up Adopted*]

What Do You Mean I Have a Learning Disability? by Kathleen M. Dwyer (Walker, 1991)

MORE PROBLEM SOLVING TIPS

Warning Signs

If your child is experiencing problems that he or she is having difficulty solving or talking about, you may begin to notice warning signs:

- getting in trouble/breaking rules
- emotional outbursts
- sulking
- aggression towards classmates or family members
- poor performance
- lethargy

These can be your cue to try and get your child to open up to you or to seek other help. Sometimes a brief call to your child's teacher can provide valuable insights on what might be bothering him or her. Never feel that you have to wait for a designated conference date to call your child's teacher.

If I Knew Then What I Know Now

Read these boxed words of wisdom with your child. Talk about everyday experiences each of you encounter where these words of wisdom could be applied.

Teachers have bad days, too.

You're not the only one that feels that way! Everyone feels embarrassed, confused, nervous, or frightened at some time or other.

Everyone is entitled to his or her opinion and there are many different opinions. Try to be tolerant.

It's OK to be angry, but not to hurt others.

It's OK if you don't like everyone, but treat everyone kindly and fairly anyway.

It's OK that not everyone likes you, but you have the right to be treated kindly and fairly by everyone. Unfortunately not everyone will. It's not your fault.

When you do something that you feel is dumb, you probably remember it far longer than anyone else.

SPEAKING UP

Public Speaking

As your child progresses through school, he or she will have more opportunities for speaking in front of a group, a class, or the entire school. Public speaking may be something your child excels at and enjoys. For other children, it is a frightening experience. If your child is in the latter category, you can ease his or her discomfort by providing times at home when your child can speak up in a relaxed, supportive environment.

Watch Others

Everyone has different gifts and some have the gift of speaking. Encourage your child to appreciate the talents of others and to try to recognize what makes them effective. Look and listen for gifted speakers around you or on television or film. For example, you might watch a videoclip of Martin Luther King, Jr.'s "I Have a Dream" speech. Or perhaps your minister, priest, or rabbi gives inspiring sermons. Even analyzing TV commercials can help your child see and hear effective or ineffective speech.

Oral Reports

Fifth graders are often required to give oral reports. The checklist to the right can help your child prepare if this is a new event for him or her.

Oral Report Checklist:

❒ 1. Know your topic. Research it thoroughly.

❒ 2. Be prepared. Practice what you plan to say in front of a friendly audience (Mom, Dad, your cat) or a mirror.

❒ 3. Don't try to read your speech. Write just the important points and key words on notecards. (Notecards, unlike paper, won't crinkle and shake if you are nervous.)

❒ 4. Speak slowly and clearly.

❒ 5. Speak up!

❒ 6. Use good eye contact. Each time you look up from your notes, glance at a different area of the room.

❒ 7. Look over everyone's head at a spot on the back wall if looking at the faces in your audience makes you nervous. Or pick a few friendly faces to look at.

❒ 8. Your facial expressions should match the mood of what you are saying.

❒ 9. Use proper voice inflections when excited, asking a question, or to show suspense.

❒ 10. Try to relax!

Home and School Cooperation

Forgetfulness, carelessness, messiness, distractions, daydreaming, and wasted time can all become obstacles to your child's success in school. None of these reflects your child's true intelligence, knowledge, or abilities, but they can prevent your child from making the most of his or her talents. Your child can combat all of them by getting organized.

Overall, getting organized is not a simple task, but there are many simple things that you can help your child do to work toward better organization.

GETTING ORGANIZED—ASSIGNMENTS

One of the most important responsibilities that is placed increasingly on your child as he or she progresses through school is getting assignments completed and handed in on time. The first step in accomplishing this is learning to keep track of the day's assignments. Your child may be in the habit of "remembering" what needs to be done, but at this level expectations are changing. Teachers are attempting to prepare students for the greater responsibility that will be expected of them in middle school, junior high, or high school. The assignments are becoming more numerous and more complicated. Long range assignments requiring greater planning are more common. Relying on memory alone may no longer be enough.

Some method of recording and keeping track of assignments is necessary. Help your child find the method best suited to him or her.

- **Assignment notebooks** are a common solution, however, the small ones are lost, misplaced, or forgotten easily. Designating a standard size notebook as an assignment notebook may work better.
- **Weekly assignment sheets** are an even better solution, especially when they are attached to a pocket folder or a manila envelope in which the completed work can be stored. The sheet should have main headings for each subject area followed by subheadings for each day of the week or it could have days of the week as main headings followed by the different subject areas.
- An **assignment calendar** may also work, but may not provide enough space to adequately describe each assignment. These must be maintained for a longer period of time also which allows greater opportunity for losing it.

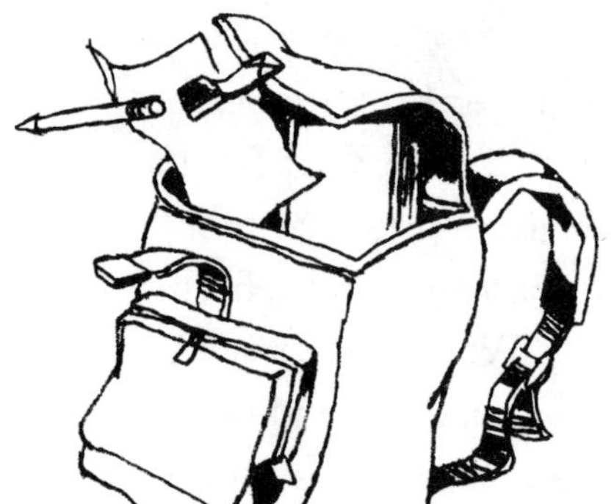

GETTING IT STRAIGHT

Listening carefully, following directions, and asking questions when he or she doesn't understand can help your child to be more organized from the very beginning of an assignment. Your child will waste far less time starting over and redoing work.

MORE ORGANIZATION TIPS

Encourage your child to give you advance notice when he or she is running low on an item.

Be Prepared

Encourage your child to pack up homework as soon as it is done to avoid misplacing it and to keep it out of the reach of younger siblings and pets. Have your child pack his or her backpack and pick out clothes for the next day before bedtime. He or she will be less rushed and better able to remember what is needed than in the morning.

Most teachers provide a list of necessary supplies at the beginning of the school year. The list can be readily filled at the many back-to-school sales. Help your child to maintain his or her supply of materials throughout the year by replacing used up or lost items promptly.

DISTRACTIONS, DISTRACTIONS

The school supply aisles in the weeks preceding the start of school contain an avalanche of materials for cutting, coloring, carrying, clipping, and clanking your child's way through class. Fight the temptations and stick to the teacher's list. Avoid unnecessary gadgets and gizmos and otherwise cumbersome items. They will only serve to distract your child and get in the way. Remember, the school desks are only so big.

Talk to your child about using time wisely in school and avoiding the many other distractions. The less time your child spends fidgeting, daydreaming, or gazing around the room or out the window, the less time he or she will need to spend finishing the work as homework later. Help your child see that distractions at home such as TV, phone calls, games, and comics break the concentration and make it necessary for him or her to start over the process of organizing thoughts for school work.

THE CLEAN SWEEP

Lack of organization can make your child's day a game of "Lost and Found." Valuable class time is wasted each day while students try to locate their completed work. Many a poor grade has been the result of assignments that have been completed, but that cannot be found.

Help your child to realize the importance of straightening his or her desk often and cleaning out the backpack daily. Encourage your child to avoid loose papers which are easily crumpled, torn, or misplaced. These simple steps will help your child sidestep the lost and found trap.

GETTING IT DONE

Getting work in on time will help your child avoid getting caught in the spiral of late and incomplete assignments. Staying organized and on top of things is far better than always trying to catch up.

Reading to gather and retain information takes concentration and some sort of organized approach.

A Study Tip

Learning the mechanics of reading does not guarantee that your child will be able to read effectively in the content areas. Several systems have been suggested to help students in this area. Here are two you may want to introduce to help your child make the most of study time.

The first is SQ3R which stands for Survey-Question-Read-Recite-Review. When your child comes home with a reading assignment, suggest that he or she first briefly look over the assigned pages. Your child should skim headings, boldfaced words, italics, graphs, illustration captions, and the end-of-the-chapter questions. It should only take a few minutes, but will give your child a good idea of what he or she will be reading. Next, your child should ask what he or she expects to learn by reading the pages. These first two steps will help your child focus on the assignment and read with greater understanding. When your child has completed the reading, he or she should attempt to put the main points into his or her own words either verbally or in writing. Your child can now review the material quite easily by reading the notes or by again skimming the assigned pages.

K-W-L is a more recent variation of this system. Before reading or studying a topic, students list what they already know (K) about the topic. They also list what they want (W) to know about the topic. Afterwards they list what they have learned (L).

Research Tip

Whether your child is faced with the traditional card catalog or a newer computerized cataloging system at the library, you can make this suggestion. If your child is trying to find information on a particular topic, have him or her locate several books and their call numbers using the catalog system. This will tell your child where the books on that topic are located in the library. He or she can then go to the "stacks" or shelves and look through the actual books on the topic deciding which will be helpful. It is much easier to make selections when looking at the books, which allows for skimming and looking through contents and indexes, rather than just looking at the limited information in the card catalog.

A CHECKLIST FOR TEST-TAKING:

- ❒ 1. Be prepared. Worry less and study more.
- ❒ 2. Get to bed on time the night before.
- ❒ 3. Eat a good breakfast the morning of the test.
- ❒ 4. Don't "cram" minutes before the test. It will only confuse you.
- ❒ 5. Skim the test so you can pace yourself properly.
- ❒ 6. Read directions carefully before you begin.
- ❒ 7. Keep your eyes on your own work.
- ❒ 8. If you are not sure of an answer, go with your first instinct.
- ❒ 9. Write neatly.
- ❒ 10. Answer every question, even if you are not sure.
- ❒ 11. Check over your work before handing it in. Be sure that you have answered every question.

A CHECKLIST FOR NOTE-TAKING:

- ❒ 1. Notes help you remember the main ideas and important details. Use only key words and phrases when taking notes.
- ❒ 2. Put notes in your own words so you will understand them better.
- ❒ 3. Boldface, italics, and pictures are clues to what the author felt was important. Look for those items when taking notes.
- ❒ 4. Reread your notes soon after taking them to fill in points you may have forgotten.
- ❒ 5. Rewrite your notes to help you remember them.

The Benefits Abound

A good homework program can help your child build better study habits and a sense of responsibility. It can provide extension of the ideas and further practice of skills covered in the classroom. It can teach your child to organize his or her time more wisely. It can give your child opportunities to follow directions and complete work independently.

While the value of these aspects of homework would probably not be argued, the practice of assigning homework may still be controversial with some parents and certainly some students who feel that they have put in a long enough day at school and that they deserve a rest in the after-school hours. Even in households that are pro-homework, the subject may still be a serious source of controversy between parents and children. How can parents help their children reap all the benefits of homework without all the friction and frustration? Specific ground rules and guidelines are a good first step.

A Homework Policy

It is very helpful to find out early in the year if your child's school or individual teachers have a set homework policy. This will give you an idea of what to expect. Sometimes this is done through a statement in a school handbook or a letter from your child's teacher. If this is not the case, you may need to contact your child's teacher and ask.

It's About Time; It's About Space

Once you have determined the type of homework to expect, it is good to set a specific time that will be reserved each day or night for homework. Even on days when there is no homework, use this time for some type of reading, drill, or practice to help establish the homework routine. Use a commercial game like Scrabble that reinforces a skill, yet is enjoyable, for a no homework night.

Next, designate a suitable work area. Choose a place where your child can work free from noise and distractions such as TV, siblings, or pets. It doesn't need to be a special desk. It might just be a corner of the kitchen counter or dining room table reserved and kept clear for your child.

Let Your Child in on Decisions

At this age you may want your child to help choose the homework time that is best. Would your child prefer a break first or would he or she rather get homework over with right away, leaving the rest of the evening clear? Experiment with different times at the beginning of the year to help find the ideal time.

The more responsibility you can place on your child for decisions concerning homework, the less you will find yourself in the position of being the "Homework Sheriff."

HOMEWORK TIPS

Getting Started

To help your child remember the time on his or her own, make a sign that says, for example "Homework—5:30" and post it in an obvious spot. Try signing a simple contract with your child to give him or her more of a feeling of commitment to the routine.

Pacing

Help your child to estimate the amount of time he or she will need to complete an assignment. Encourage your child to think ahead and avoid leaving five minutes of work time for a half hour of homework. For long range assignments, help your child to spread the work out over several nights rather than saving it all for the night before it is due.

Avoid Overscheduling

Be sure that your child has time left for homework. Avoid overscheduling after-school activities. It may be disappointing making your child choose between extracurricular activities, but it will pay off later when you and your child are both faced with less frustration.

Dictionary Dilemma

Try to have a junior dictionary available at home for your child's use. College dictionaries or adult level dictionaries often have definitions that are more difficult for your young student to understand than the word that originally gave him or her trouble.

Avoiding the Stall

Have all the necessary supplies close at hand. Place them in a shoebox, basket, old tackle box, nearby drawer, or any of a variety of plastic storage boxes or caddies available at discount stores. Produce this at homework time and avoid the common excuses for wandering and stalling.

Homework Supplies:

- **sharpened pencils**
- **erasers**
- **pencil sharpener**
- **pens**
- **highlighter**
- **crayons, markers, or colored pencils**
- **lined writing paper**
- **blank paper**
- **scissors**
- **tape**
- **glue**
- **ruler (inches and centimeters)**
- **calculator**
- **dictionary**

A HEALTHY HELPING OF HOMEWORK HELP

Stay Close

Determine how your child performs best—alone or with help, with soft music or without. At this age it is not uncommon for children to let you know loud and clear that they would rather do it themselves. Either way, try to be nearby so you are "available for questioning." Use this time to do your work as well. Read a book or magazine, write a letter, balance your checkbook, or write out bills. Even if your child doesn't need you, he or she won't feel as left out or isolated from the rest of the family.

Correction, Please

Resist the urge to correct your child's homework unless the teacher has requested that you do so. Even though you may feel it will reflect poorly on you as a parent if your child returns with a less than perfect homework sheet, the teacher may actually prefer that you not correct the work. Seeing your child's errors is helpful in diagnosing problem areas he or she may have. Let your child know that you won't be correcting the work and why, but by all means, show an interest and look over it when finished. If you absolutely can't resist, zero in on a few mistakes and ask your child questions about how he or she arrived at the answers. But do not make the corrections for your child. Let your child try again and he or she may catch some careless mistakes. For spelling errors, make a list of correct spellings on a separate sheet of paper. Let your child proofread the writing to find and correct the misspellings. This not only gets your child to look at his or her own work more closely, but helps you avoid marking up the paper which can be very upsetting.

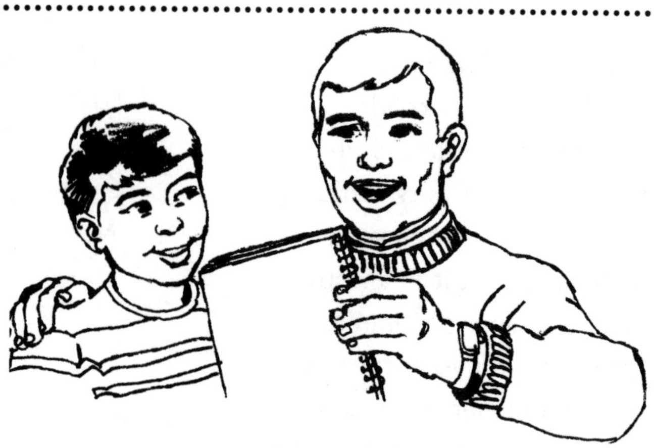

Don't Over Do It

Be helpful, but don't become overly involved. If your child seems to be having trouble getting started, help him or her read through the directions as a first step. Often failure to read or understand the directions is the main stumbling block. Once your child gets started, back off. Offer help only when asked and maybe a few restrained reminders about neatness if you really can't help yourself.

Outside Help May Be the Answer

Sometimes your fifth-grade child will be resistant to your attempts at helping no matter what approach you take. Try enlisting the help of a babysitter, an elderly neighbor, or one of your child's peers when drilling and practicing spelling words or math facts. When encountering other stumbling blocks, make use of a homework hotline if one is available in your area.

Avoid New Approaches

Try to feel out the approach the teacher is using and avoid confusing your child by offering new strategies.

MORE HOMEWORK TIPS

Rewards

Offering rewards for completing homework may be criticized as bribing, but it can also be looked at as the positive reinforcement necessary to avoid the use of punishments or negative steps later. Adults work for praise, recognition, promotions, authority, and paychecks even if they have accepted the responsibility of going to work every day. A small, short-term reward may prove to be a more tangible incentive than the grade your child will receive for completing the work or the knowledge that he or she has acted responsibly. These simple rewards may also seem more attainable from a child's viewpoint.

Let your child decorate any empty can or jar. Together cut out strips of heavy paper and write a reward on each. Rewards might be a chance to pick a meal, extra TV time, a can of soda, permission to stay up an extra 15 minutes, a backrub, or playing a game with you. Place all the strips in the can and let your child pick one if he or she completes the homework in the allotted time without a fuss.

Bookmarks

The bookmarks on pages 69 and 70 can be used as rewards or in other ways including those listed to the right.

Warnings

You may want to check with the teacher if your child continually comes home without homework, especially now that he or she is in the intermediate grades. Your child may in truth not have homework, but may be rushing through it on the bus or at other times and doing an inadequate job which could adversely affect his or her grades.

It may also be helpful to determine whether the work your child brings home was assigned as homework or was classwork that was not completed in class. If it is incomplete classwork, it may mean your child is having difficulty academically or is not using the time in class wisely.

Sometimes homework may be forgotten "accidentally-on-purpose." Avoid letting this become a habit by making your child do an alternate assignment during homework time. The actual assignment will still have to be done, but in the meantime your child hasn't succeeded in getting out of any work.

Bookmark Rewards

- **Give one to your child at the beginning of a project as motivation, during a project as encouragement to continue, or as a reward for the completion of a project.**
- **Include them in birthday cards or as stocking stuffers for the holidays. Or slip one in a lunchbag or backpack as a surprise.**
- **Tape one to the mirror to start the day positively.**
- **Give your child one after a long day or week.**
- **Give your child one for bringing home a good grade or a neater paper than usual.**
- **Use them to reward your child for studying hard for a test or working hard on a project regardless of the resulting grade.**

COMMUNICATING WITH YOUR CHILD

Your child hops on that big yellow bus in the morning and disappears down the road. You don't see your child again until late afternoon when the bus again rolls up to your house and out he or she jumps. Is what has gone on during those seven to eight hours like a giant, black hole, lost forever? You are fairly certain that your child hasn't spent the last eight hours doing "nothin'," but how can you get your child to give you more than a shrug and a one-word answer?

There are certain attitudes that will naturally foster communication.

Attitudes

Respect, approval, honesty, acceptance, encouragement, support, appreciation, and a focus on strengths and accomplishments are attitudes you should strive for in dealing with your child if you expect him or her to feel comfortable communicating with you. This doesn't mean that you must approve and accept everything that your child says or does. This could be more harmful than poor communication. Rather, strive to see and acknowledge behaviors in your child that are deserving of these attitudes and work towards making these your natural reactions.

Attitudes that hinder communication are criticizing, belittling, judging, preaching, lecturing, talking down to, pointing out faults, blaming, shaming, and ridiculing. Sometimes you may exhibit some of these attitudes without realizing it out of exhaustion, frustration, or lack of time. You may even be expressing them without ever saying a word through your facial expressions or body language.

Try to speak to your child the way you expect your child to speak to you and other people. Try to speak to your child the way you would speak to others.

Be willing to admit to your child when you have not acted appropriately. When you lose your temper, try to apologize to your child once you have calmed down. Tell your child his or her behavior was still not acceptable, but that your reaction to it was also wrong. Compare it to a tantrum and let your child know that it is something that you too must work on. It is often surprising how supportive and forgiving children can be when they are spoken to in an honest and respectful manner.

Active Listening

Active listening is a way of showing acceptance and understanding while listening to your child, without being judgmental or giving advice. It involves paraphrasing what your child has said and then listening again and giving your child time to continue and build on his or her thoughts. It is not merely parroting the words, but restating them in your own words so that your child knows that you understand him or her. It may seem odd at first, but you will be surprised by how much it can help your child to open up.

Open-ended Questions

It is also important to try and use open-ended questions with your child if you want to encourage further communication. This means avoiding questions that can be answered with one word like, "Did you have a good day at school?" You should also try to avoid questions that are too broad or general like, "What did you learn today?" Although it is a valuable question, it may take too much thought or require such a lengthy response that your child won't feel like going into it and instead you'll get, "Nothin'." Ask specific questions, such as "What did you do in science today?" or "What was the best thing that happened today?"

I-Messages

Using I-messages is another strategy for building more positive communication. It is a way of avoiding placing value judgments on your child's behavior or placing blame on him or her for how you feel. Rather than starting with phrases like "You make me so angry", "You never do what you are told" or "You are so careless . . . messy . . . sassy . . ." that criticize or place blame, try starting with phrases that express how your child's behavior makes you feel, without alienating or labeling your child. Show disapproval of the behavior, not the child. Until it becomes more natural, try remembering the following pattern:

I feel ***frustrated*** *when you* ***leave your room a mess*** *because* ***it makes more work for me.***

I feel (emotion) when you (behavior) because (consequence or result).

Read On

If you are interested in reading more about these and other strategies, the following books are helpful:

***Parent Effectiveness Training* by Tom Gordon (Peter H. Wyden, 1970)**

***How To Talk So Kids Will Listen and Listen So Kids Will Talk* by Adele Faber and Elaine Mazlish (Avon Books, 1980)**

***Kids Are Worth It! Giving Your Child the Gift of Inner Discipline* by Barbara Coloroso (Morrow, 1994)**

COMMUNICATION SUGGESTIONS

Start when your child is young. Then it will be easier to talk to him or her later when the issues become more serious.

Be sure to talk to your child about positive topics. If the only time you talk to your child is when there is a problem, he or she is bound to start avoiding conversations with you.

Try and listen when your child does talk, no matter how long it takes him or her to get around to the point. The most valuable communication often comes up while engaged in ordinary day-to-day activities rather than at a pre-scheduled discussion time.

Make your conversations two-way. Be willing to share information about your day or yourself. A good conversation should involve listening and talking, asking and telling.

Try to pick a good time and place for communication. This will not be the same for every child. For some the best time might be right after school when issues are fresh in their minds. Others may not feel like rehashing their day so soon, but need a break first. Dinnertime or bedtime might work for some. If there are younger siblings and generally lots of commotion, you may want to purposely arrange some time alone without the other siblings and distractions. A bike ride, a walk, or even a trip to the grocery store may be good opportunities for talk.

Focus on effort or accomplishments rather than on labeling. A negative label may be hard to live down, but a positive label may seem hard to live up to and can be equally frightening to your child. Say, "What an exciting story!" rather than, "You are quite an author!"

Deal with questions as they arise and don't feel that you have to cover every aspect of a topic once it is brought up. Just give your child the information that he or she asks for at the time. Let your child absorb it and come back with further questions.

PARENT-TEACHER CONFERENCES

Most schools have specially designated conference days once or twice a year. Generally they will be held at the end of a grading period, in conjunction with report card distribution. They are usually limited to 15 minutes in length, but those 15 minutes can cause anxiety for your child, yourself, and even your child's teacher. Your child is nervous because your child realizes that he or she is the topic of discussion. You may be nervous because you fear your child isn't where he or she should be academically or socially. Your child's teacher is nervous because he is or she is about to discuss a topic with you that is closest to your heart, your child, without necessarily knowing how defensive or supportive you will be.

WHAT THE TEACHER BRINGS TO THE CONFERENCE

In addition to any specific problem areas your child may be facing, the teacher can be expected to provide some more general information concerning test scores, classroom grades, social development, attitude and behavior, work samples, and upcoming material to be covered—all in 15 minutes.

QUESTIONS PARENTS SHOULD ASK

- Ask which subjects your child does best in and which he or she does the worst in according to the teacher's observations. Do these coincide with your own observations?
- Ask what additional enrichment or help you can give your child outside of the classroom.
- Ask about your child's class participation.
- Ask about your child's friendships, interactions with friends, and choice of friends.
- Ask about your child's strengths and weaknesses in areas other than academics.
- Ask if the teacher feels your child is working up to his or her ability. Is your child motivated?
- Ask how your child interacts with adults in the school setting.

- Ask about the teacher's policies on homework, late work, make-up work, grading, corrections, extra credit, class participation, book reports, or independent reading if you have concerns in any of these areas.

CONFERENCE TIPS

Knowing that all parties involved are in the same boat and hopefully on the same team, what can be done to help make the conference as productive as possible?

1. Get to know your child's teacher prior to the conference date to help ease the anxiety at conference time. You may be able to introduce yourself at an open house or other school event or you may be able to make a few casual visits to your child's classroom.

2. Before going to the conference, give some consideration to completed work and homework that your child has brought home. Bring along any that have raised questions in your mind. Page through some of the textbooks. Think about your child's strengths and weaknesses and how he or she reacts to different situations. Doing this may suggest some questions you would like to ask at the conference. It may also bring to mind some information that could add to the teacher's understanding of your child.

3. Discuss the conference with your child prior to attending. Try to ask specific questions like, "What is your favorite subject this year? your worst? Have you had any problems with classes? teachers? friends?" Questions that are too general like, "Is there anything you want me to mention at the conference?" will elicit a similarly general response. "Not really."

4. Make a list of possible questions. Time will be limited and a list can help you stay on track.

5. Be prompt. Conferences are usually scheduled back to back and being late can shorten your conference or cut into the next parent's.

6. Try to leave children at home if possible. This will allow you and your child's teacher to speak more candidly and directly without concern for your child's feelings.

7. Try to start the conference on a positive note. Offer a compliment, thank you, or a positive comment. It may pertain to something your child has told you about the teacher. It may pertain to a project he or she enjoyed or some new skill or knowledge that you have seen your child employ. Any words of praise should of course be genuine.

8. Don't be afraid to share information about family situations such as a divorce, illness, or loss that may be stressful to your child. Such situations could have adverse effects on your child's behavior or performance. The teacher may be a valuable ally in helping you to catch problems before they become more serious.

CONFERENCE FOLLOW-UP

It is important to share the results of the conference with your child especially if he or she has been waiting on pins and needles for your return. Emphasize the positive. Use discretion. Not everything you have learned needs to be shared with your child. Try to determine what information will be appropriate or helpful to him or her. It is best if your child views conferences as a show of support rather than parents and teachers ganging up on him or her.

If you are dissatisfied with the conference results or feel that a problem is not being handled appropriately, let the teacher know that you would like a second opinion or other suggestions and that you will be speaking to the principal, school psychologist, or other school personnel about the situation. The teacher may even be able to direct you. For best results, try to present this in as non-threatening a way as possible.

Try to act on any suggestions that you have received from the teacher and keep in touch with updates.

RESCHEDULING A CONFERENCE

If you are unable to come to the conference at the designated time, talk to the teacher and try to arrive at an alternate time that is agreeable to both of you. This could be before school hours, after school hours, during lunch, or at recess time. It may even be necessary to conduct the conference by telephone. Most teachers are eager to arrange some way to meet with the parents.

WHEN CONFERENCE TIME IS NOT ENOUGH

If you have more questions than the scheduled conference time will permit, don't be afraid to request an additional conference time at some other time.

Never try to conduct a conference when other students are present or at a social event. It is far more productive to set up an appointment with the teacher so he or she can have the necessary materials and information available.

VOLUNTEERS, PLEASE!

Although most parents would probably agree that their child's teacher could use some help, classroom volunteers are a rarity. Some parents are intimidated by the school setting because of their own past school encounters. Some may feel they are not qualified to make any beneficial contribution. Still others may feel at a loss for time because they hold a full-time job themselves or have small children at home. Several important facts should put all these reservations to rest.

Ask the Teacher

There are ways to use everyone's talents. If you are unsure of what you have to offer, make your desire to help known to the teacher and ask for suggestions. Tell the teacher which areas you would feel most comfortable with. If you have a specific activity in mind, be sure to communicate that.

Help on a Regular Basis

A few hours a week or a month committed to assisting in the classroom can be very valuable to a teacher who is stretched thin in a classroom of 25 or more students. This time can be spent listening to students read, drilling math facts, working on spelling words and vocabulary, helping students with make-up work, listening to oral book reports, or assisting with an art or science project that requires additional guidance.

Help on an Occasional Basis

If you are available on a more limited basis, you may be able to chaperone a field trip, supervise during a class party, present a holiday project, offer to read to the class, or be a guest speaker telling about your job, a special trip, a talent, or a hobby.

For those who cannot make it in to the classroom, there are still numerous options:

Help From Home or Your Workplace

- Use your organizational skills by making phone calls, typing, or preparing materials for class projects while at home.
- Let the teacher know if there are books, posters, or artifacts that you have and are willing to share that might relate to a unit of study.
- Make yourself available for evening activities sponsored by your school such as book fairs and sports events.
- If nothing else, paying dues to your local parent organization or participating in local fund raisers will help supply the resources necessary to allow others to help.

A joy that's shared is a joy made double. —English Proverb

Yard by yard,
it's very hard.
But inch by inch,
it's a cinch.

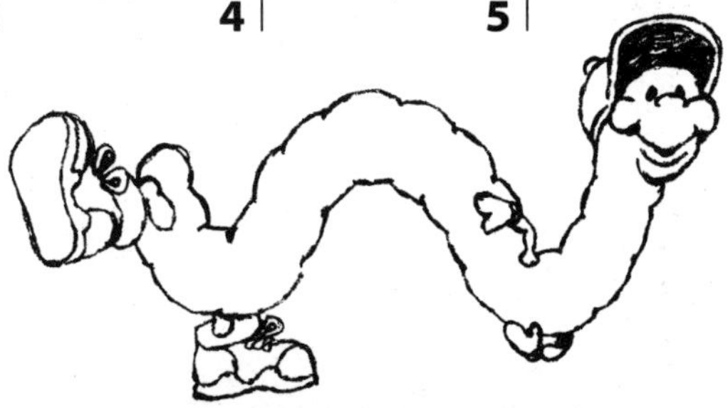

I am a slow walker,
but I never walk back.
—Abraham Lincoln

Everybody
knows
more than
somebody,
but **nobody**
knows
more than
everybody.

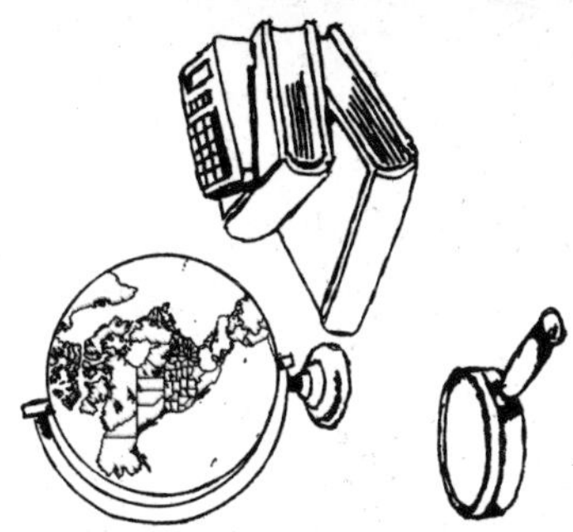

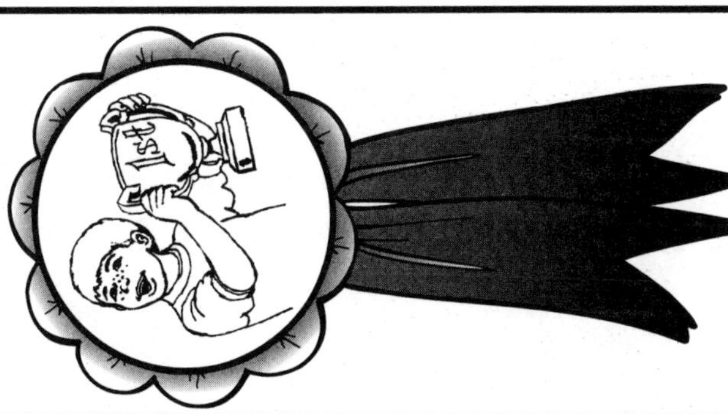

A winner
never quits,
and a quitter
never wins.

Backs of Bookmarks

What Have You Read Lately?

Worksheet

What is the best book you've read in the past six weeks?

Title ________________________________

Author ________________________________

On a scale of 1 to 10 (10 is best), how would you rate this book? Why? Rating ________ Reasoning ________________

____

____

To whom would you recommend this book? Why do you think that person would like it? ________________

____

____

____

What book have you read lately that you thought was OK, but not great?

Title ________________________________

____

Author ________________________________

On a scale of 1 to 10 (10 is best), how would you rate this book? Why?

Rating ________ Reasoning ________________

____

____

How would you change the book to make it better? ________________

____

____

____

Building Better Stories

Worksheet

Just as you need all the ingredients to bake a good cake, you need all the right ingredients to write a good story. Read about five of these story elements.

Characters: the people or animals that the story is about

Setting: when and where the story takes place

Conflict: the problem, the main source of tension and drama

Climax: the most important and emotional part when the action is the greatest; it usually comes near or at the end

Resolution: the ending, including the solution to the problem

Use your imagination and fill in the missing story elements for each of these world–record holders. Then choose one and write the story.

1. Character: Charles Osborne from Iowa hiccuped for 69 years and 5 months.

Setting: ______________________________

Conflict: ______________________________

Climax: ______________________________

Resolution: ______________________________

2. Character: In 1986, "Chu Lin," a giant panda living at the zoo in Madrid, Spain, was valued at $1.4 million.

Setting: ______________________________

Conflict: ______________________________

Climax: ______________________________

Resolution: ______________________________

3. Character: Australian Neville Patten owns the smallest ridable bicycle. Its wheels measure 0.76 inches in diameter and he rode it for 13 feet 5½ inches.

Setting: ______________________________

Conflict: ______________________________

Climax: ______________________________

Resolution: ______________________________

Encyclopedia Search

Worksheet

This encyclopedia is divided into 22 volumes.

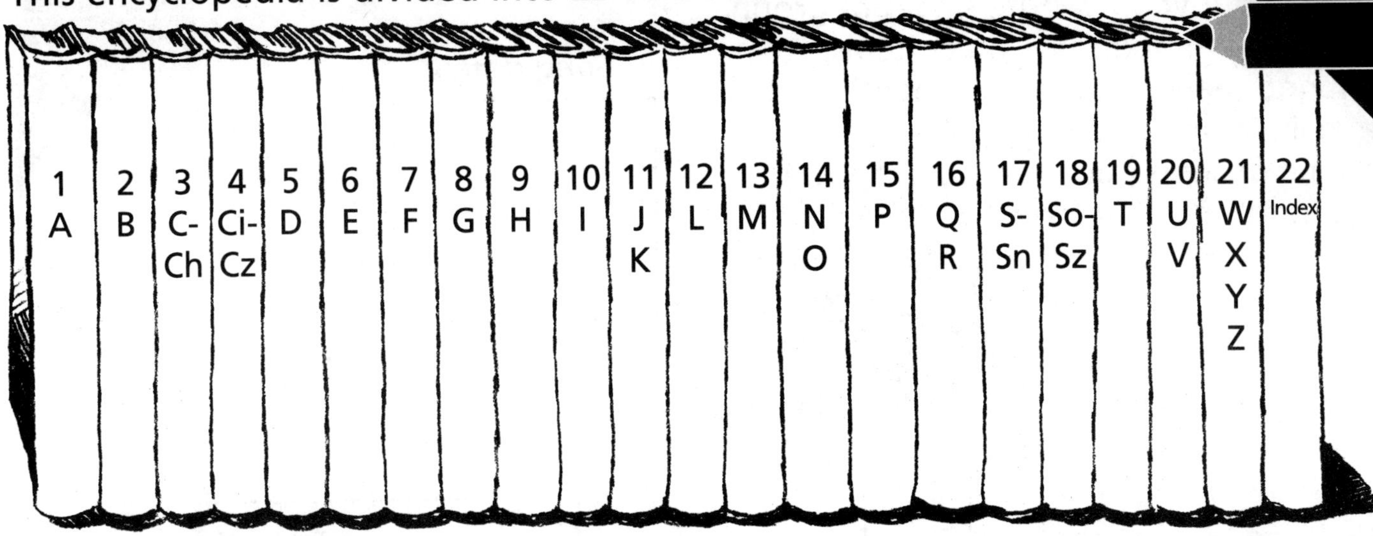

Give the volume number in which you would find each of these topics.

teeth ________ horse ________
metric system ________ kite flying ________
vaccines ________ agriculture ________
Wisconsin ________ Canada ________
space travel ________ pollution ________
Montana ________ dinosaur ________
school ________ Constitution ________
Phoenix ________ anteater ________

Name a topic you'd expect to find in each volume below.

Volume 3 ____________________ Volume 13 ____________________
Volume 8 ____________________ Volume 18 ____________________
Volume 1 ____________________ Volume 20 ____________________

Sometimes it helps to look up a few different words to find information about your topic. Read these topics. Write a related word or phrase you could try looking up.

Jupiter ____________________ slavery ____________________
Pablo Picasso ____________________ Big Dipper ____________________
ostrich ____________________ violin ____________________

Get Caught in a Web!

Worksheet

A web helps you organize information. Finish this web about your favorite singer or group. Song details might include these items:

- the mood (happy, sad, silly, romantic . . .)
- the main idea of the song
- the type of song (rock, rap, country . . .)
- the cassette or CD it is on
- the instruments played

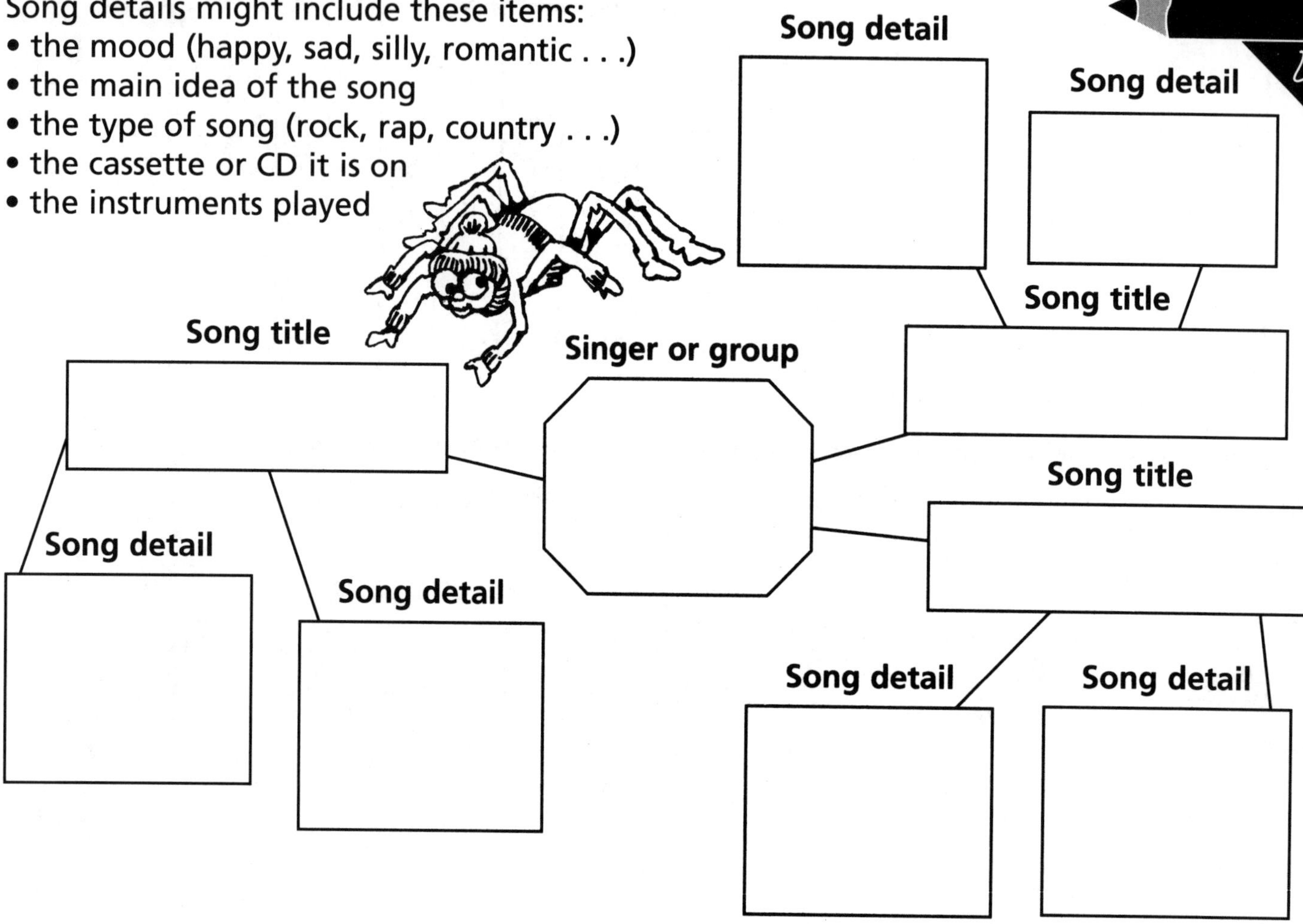

Now create an outline. The singer or group can be the main topic (I). The songs can be the subtopics (A, B, C). Information about each song can be listed as details under the song titles (1, 2).

I. ____________________

  A. ____________________

    1. ____________________

    2. ____________________

  B. ____________________

    1. ____________________

    2. ____________________

  C. ____________________

    1. ____________________

    2. ____________________

Think About It!
How is your web like your outline? How is it different?

Ads or Adds?

Worksheet

Read each of the riddles below.
Write the correct homonym on the line next to it.

1. What section of the newspaper does a math teacher like best? (The classified "adds.") ____________

2. Why did the librarian get fired? (He told the students there was no reading "allowed" in the library.) ____________

3. Do you know why the teacher "paste" the floor? (She wanted to stick to the basics.) ____________

4. Why did the music class put their instruments away? (The music teacher said he had "banned" practice that afternoon.) ____________

5. Why did the science teacher put price tags on her pea plants? (She wanted to see a plant "sell.") ____________

6. Why was the student so up-tight before the test? (He forgot what he'd been "taut.") ____________

7. Why did the gym class forget to run around the track? (They had memory "laps.") ____________

List 10 other homonym pairs. Write your own riddle using one of them.

____

____

____

____

____

Riddle: ____________________

____

____

Answer: ____________________

____

____

____

You Name the Game

Worksheet

Set Up:

Write vocabulary words you need to study on separate cards.
Number each card 1, 2, or 3.
Find coins, buttons, or other objects for playing pieces.

How to Play:

1. Mix up the cards and place them facedown in a pile. The first player picks a card, reads the word, and tells its meaning. The player then moves the matching number of spaces (1, 2, or 3) and does the activity on the game board below. Then his or her turn is over.
2. Take turns and continue playing until one player reaches Finish.
3. Any player may challenge an answer. The challenger must find the correct answer in a dictionary or textbook. If successful, the challenger moves his or her marker the number of spaces on the card and follows the directions on the game board. Play continues with whomever's regular turn it is, another player or the challenger.

Start	Take an extra turn.	Tell what part of speech your word is.	Use your word in a sentence.	Find your word in a dictionary or textbook.
Move ahead two extra spaces.	Join any other player in his or her space.	Name a word that comes before your word in ABC order.	Spell your word without looking.	Lose a turn.
Spell your word backwards.	Write your word with the hand you usually don't write with.	Go back to Start.	Name a word that comes after your word in ABC order.	Invite another player to join you in your space.
Finish	Name another word that means about the same as your word.	Spell another word using letters from your word.	Act out your word.	Make up a rhyme using your word.

Dear Friend

Worksheet

Oops! These kids forgot to proofread their letters. Can you find and correct the errors?

Each letter has these mistakes:

- ☐ 10 capitalization errors
- ☐ 3 missing commas
- ☐ 2 missing periods
- ☐ 1 missing question mark

8691 W mulberry rd.
greenfield wi 53220
November 19 1997

Dear shana

How are you I am fine. I hope that you are fine, too.

I'm sorry I haven't written sooner, but I've been very busy

the weather here is fine.

please write back.

sincerely,
leslie

8691 s. 93rd st
sun prairie, WI 53590
november 19 1997

dear Scott

we picked our soccer teams for gym today and played our first game. Our dribbling needs some work, but we won the game anyway. Are you playing soccer at school now

It's been snowing almost every day this week. There's a big hill on the playground and at recess we can slide on it If it gets below zero, we have to stay inside for recess and play games in our classroom. I'd rather go outside!

In science we're making cardboard skeletons because we are studying muscles and bones. my group is making a caribou. It looks more like Halloween than Thanksgiving with all the skeletons hanging around.

I'll see you at Grandma's at thanksgiving.

Friend and cousin
chase

Think About It!

Which letter do you think is more interesting? Why?

Animal Analogies

Worksheet

Analogies deal with the relationships between words. A pair of words that go together in some way are grouped and compared to another pair of words that go together in the same way. For example, ant is to insect as sea gull is to bird is an analogy. Insect and bird both describe the kind of animal that each word is paired with (ant and sea gull).

Read the beginning of each analogy below. Circle the pair of words that is related in the same way.

fur is to squirrel as	feather is to bird wing is to bird
tadpole is to frog as	caterpillar is to cocoon caterpillar is to butterfly
den is to bear as	hive is to bee honey is to bee
lamb is to sheep as	fawn is to deer hare is to rabbit
lion is to savannah as	whale is to waves whale is to ocean
mammal is to giraffe as	reptile is to turtle spider is to insect
spot is to leopard as	black is to skunk stripe is to tiger
kangaroo is to hop as	dolphin is to smooth dolphin is to swim
fish is to pelican as	grass is to rhinoceros horn is to rhinoceros
rattlesnake is to desert as	chimpanzee is to primate chimpanzee is to forest

Now write some animal analogies of your own.

__________ is to __________ as __________ is to __________

__________ is to __________ as __________ is to __________

__________ is to __________ as __________ is to __________

Record Breaking Math

Worksheet

Can you read and write really big numbers? Try these.
Write the numerals for each number expressed in words.

1. A string of kites were flown to a height of thirty-one thousand, nine hundred fifty-five feet. ______

2. The largest jar of jelly beans contained three hundred seventy-eight thousand jelly beans. ______

3. In 1984 Klaus Friedrich set up and toppled two hundred eighty-one thousand, five hundred eighty-one dominoes. ______

4. California leads all other states in egg production with six billion, five hundred million eggs in a year. ______

5. Twenty-nine billion, six hundred fifty-one million, eight hundred forty thousand rolls of Life Savers candy were sold between 1913 and 1980. ______

Find some really big numbers of your own in an almanac or book of records.
Write them as numbers and as words.

Number: ______

Words: ______

______

What it describes: ______

Number: ______

Words: ______

______

What it describes: ______

Solve This!

Worksheet

Read about these world records.
Write a new question to
match the information.
Then solve both problems.

Work Space

A. The longest roller coaster in the U.S. is *The Beast* at King's Island in Ohio. The total track length is 7,400 feet. *The Viper* at Six Flags Magic Mountain, in California, is only 3,830 feet long, but it turns its riders upside down seven times.

Question 1: How much longer is *The Beast* than the *Viper?*

Solution 1: ______________________

Question 2: ______________________

____

Solution 2: ______________________

B. The hair of Mata Jagdamba of India measured 166.5 inches long in 1994. The hair of Diane Witt of Massachusetts measured 12 feet 8 inches in 1993.

Question 1: How many inches long was Diane Witt's hair?

Solution 1: ______________________

Question 2: ______________________

____

Solution 2: ______________________

C. In 1985 Eddie Leven and Delphine Chra of Chicago set the record for the longest kiss. It lasted 17 days, $10\frac{1}{2}$ hours.

Question 1: How many minutes did they kiss?

Solution 1: ______________________

Question 2: ______________________

____

Solution 2: ______________________

Earn and Learn

Worksheet

Play this game to practice adding and subtracting money. Each player will need 10 pennies. All players start with an imaginary $100 and should write this amount at the top of a sheet of paper. Take turns tossing a penny onto the game board and following the directions. Play until all pennies have been tossed. The player with the most money left wins. If a player runs out of money prior to this, he or she is out.

Babysit for the neighbors. Add $12.50.	Lose your lunch money. Subtract $2.00.	Win local coloring contest. Add $25.00. 	Recycle aluminum cans. Add $6.85.
Go to the movies. Subtract $3.75.	Do extra chores. Add $3.75. 	Buy new tennis shoes. Subtract $21.99.	Return lost dog.  Receive a reward. Add $15.00.
Collect your allowance. Add $4.00.	Pay for piano music. Subtract $8.00. 	Get an after-school job. Add $8.00.	Lose your library book. Subtract $8.95.
Buy a new pair of jeans. Subtract $15.00.	Open a birthday card from grandparents. Add $10.00.	Buy an after school snack. Subtract $1.75. 	Stop at the video arcade. Subtract $4.00.
Sell flowers you planted. Add $13.75. 	Buy a new book. Subtract $2.95.	Sign up for basketball camp. Subtract $14.00.	Find cash in your jeans pocket. Add $2.00.

The Great Divide

$42 \div 6 =$ _____ $24 \div 3 =$ _____ $36 \div 9 =$ _____

$20 \div 5 =$ _____ $16 \div 8 =$ _____ $6 \div 6 =$ _____

$18 \div 2 =$ _____ $5 \div 1 =$ _____ $28 \div 4 =$ _____

$35 \div 7 =$ _____ $54 \div 6 =$ _____ $12 \div 3 =$ _____

$8 \div 4 =$ _____ $10 \div 2 =$ _____ $48 \div 8 =$ _____

$18 \div 6 =$ _____ $40 \div 5 =$ _____ $63 \div 7 =$ _____

$72 \div 8 =$ _____ $24 \div 4 =$ _____ $6 \div 2 =$ _____

$7 \div 1 =$ _____ $0 \div 9 =$ _____ $30 \div 5 =$ _____

$3\overline{)72}$ $6\overline{)96}$ $5\overline{)85}$

$2\overline{)51}$ $4\overline{)75}$ $8\overline{)99}$

$11\overline{)385}$ $29\overline{)493}$ $90\overline{)3150}$

Snack Time Fractions

Worksheet

Cross out enough of each snack to show the fraction of each snack that was eaten.

A. $\frac{3}{4}$ of the apples

B. $\frac{2}{6}$ of the bananas

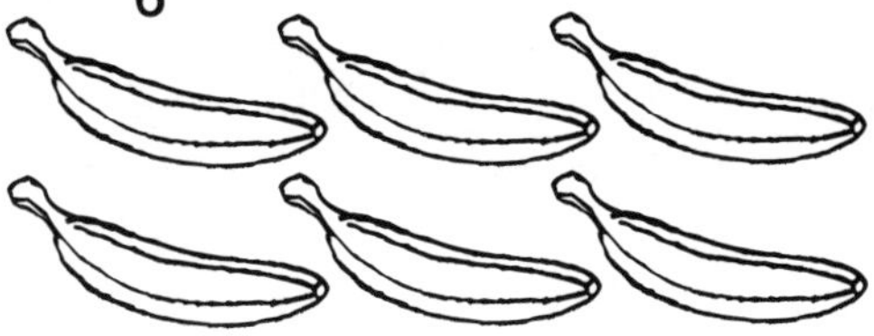

C. $\frac{1}{4}$ of the pizza

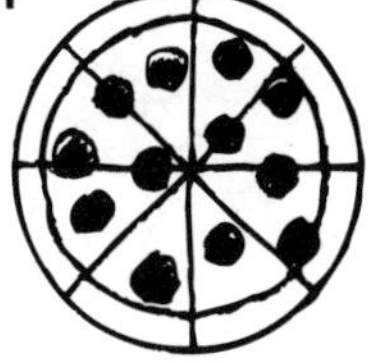

D. $\frac{2}{8}$ of the pretzels

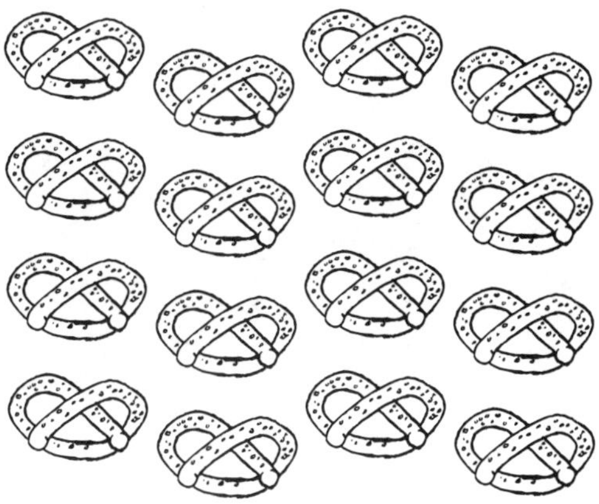

E. $\frac{1}{6}$ of the marshmallows

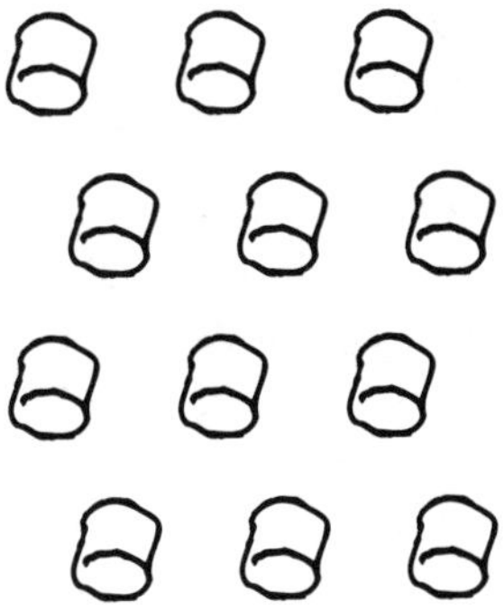

F. $\frac{2}{3}$ of the candy

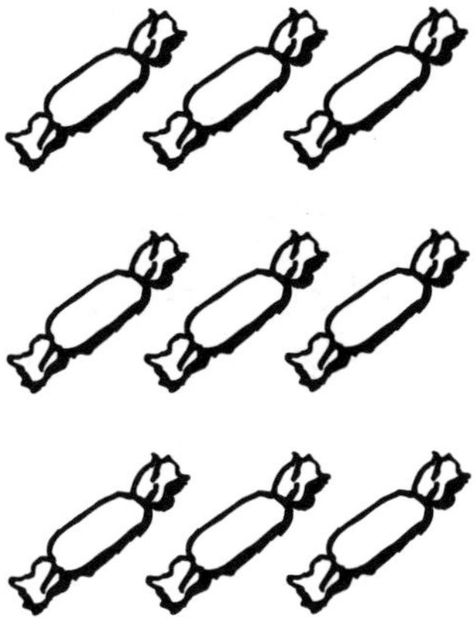

Now use the pictures above to complete the problems below.

A. $\frac{3}{4}$ of 4 = ____

$\frac{3}{4} \times \frac{4}{1}$ = ____ = ☐

B. $\frac{2}{6}$ of 6 = ____

$\frac{2}{6} \times \frac{6}{1}$ = ____ = ☐

C. $\frac{1}{4}$ of 8 = ____

$\frac{1}{4} \times \frac{8}{1}$ = ____ = ☐

D. $\frac{2}{8}$ of 16 = ____

$\frac{2}{8} \times \frac{16}{1}$ = ____ = ☐

E. $\frac{1}{6}$ of 12 = ____

$\frac{1}{6} \times \frac{12}{1}$ = ____ = ☐

F. $\frac{2}{3}$ of 9 = ____

$\frac{2}{3} \times \frac{9}{1}$ = ____ = ☐

Weather Watch

Worksheet

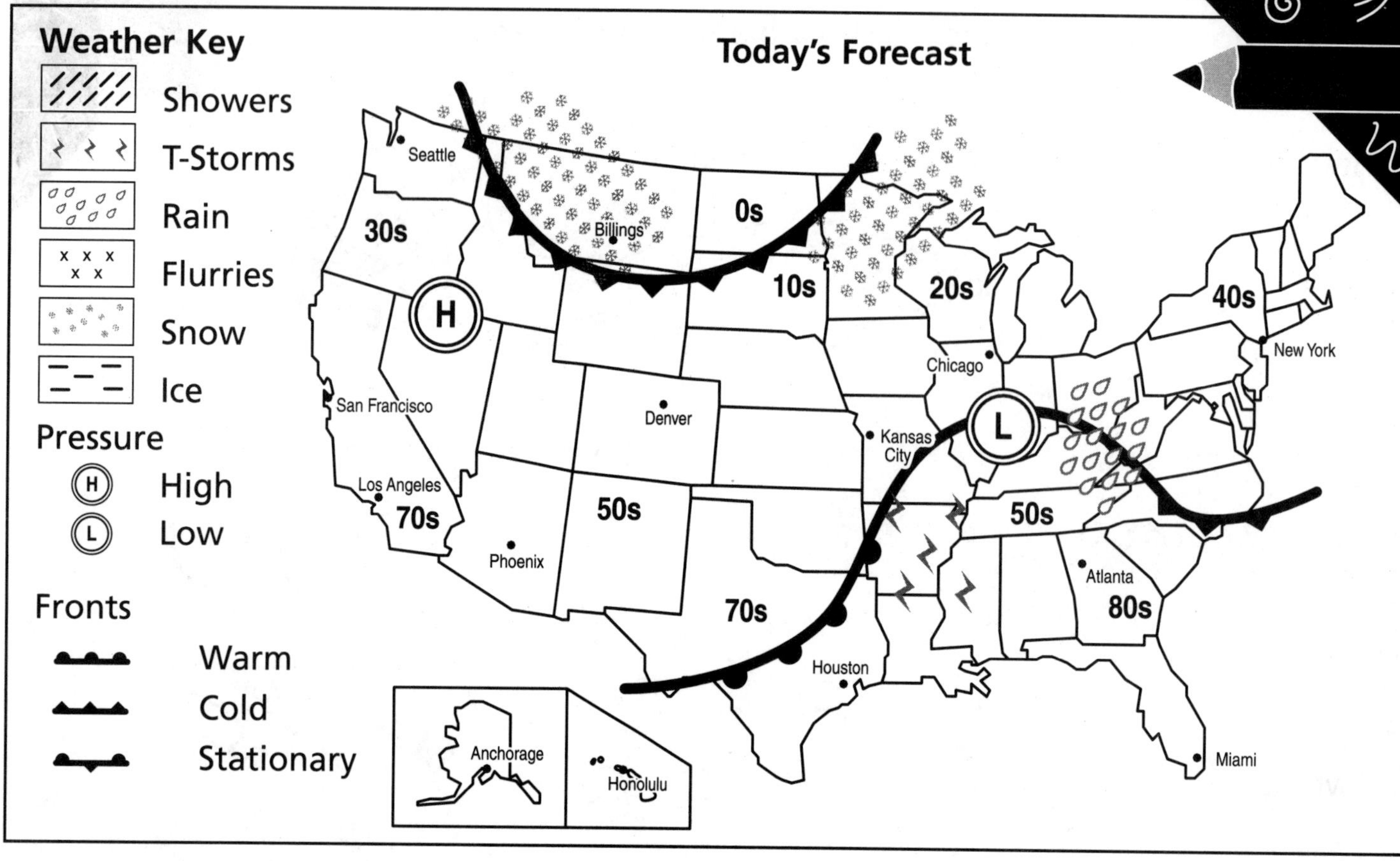

Use the weather map and key to complete these items.

1. What is the forecasted high temperature for Miami? ____________________

2. What is the forecasted low temperature for Chicago? ____________________

3. What type of precipitation is expected in Billings? ____________________

4. What type of weather is expected in Atlanta? ____________________

5. Draw rain around the San Francisco area.

6. List three states that have a cold front passing through. ____________________

____

7. Study the map. A high pressure area usually means clear weather. Do you think it also means the temperatures will be warm? Why or why not? ____________________

____

Keep a weather log for one week. Read or watch a weather forecast for your area. Look for high and low pressure areas, fronts passing through, expected precipitation, and expected high and low temperatures. Each day record the forecast and your actual weather observations. Compare the two. Were the forecasts accurate?

Plant Puzzlers

Worksheet

Use the codes found in each sentence to unlock some important information about plants. To break the code, imagine that you are turning the pointer in the center to the left or right the correct number of clicks. For example, L2 would be left two notches to the letter B.

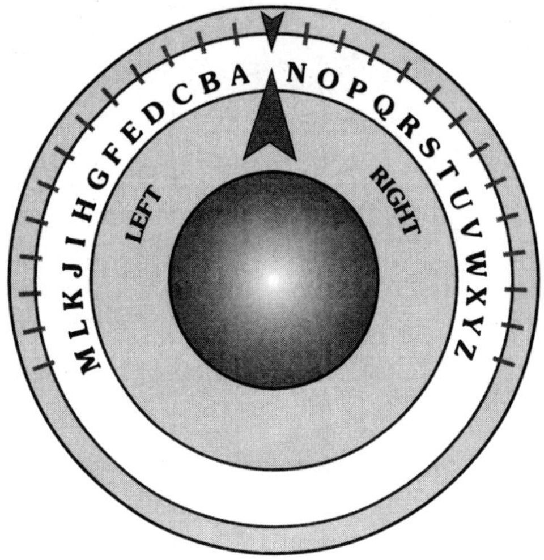

1. L2-R2-R7-L1-R1-R12 is the study of plants. ____________________

2. L13-R2-R1-R2-L3-R2-R7-R6 are seeds in which the embryo has only one main part. ____________________

3. L4-L9-L3-R2-R7-R6 are seeds in which the embryo has two main parts. ____________________

4. L1-R1-R1-R8-L1-L12-R6 are flowering plants that complete their life cycle in one year. ____________________

5. L2-L9-L5-R1-R1-L9-L1-L12-R6 are flowering plants that complete their life cycle in two years. ____________________

6. R3-L5-R5-L5-R1-R1-L9-L1-L12-R6 are flowering plants that live for more than two years. ____________________

7. L4-L5-L3-L9-L4-R8-R2-R8-R6 trees lose their leaves in fall and grow new ones in spring. ____________________

8. R7-R5-L1-R1-R6-R3-L9-R5-L1-R7-L9-R2-R1 is the giving off of water by the leaves of a plant. ____________________

Looking for Vertebrates

Find and observe a vertebrate for each group—birds, mammals, reptiles, amphibians, and fish. You may want to visit a zoo or pet shop. Then look up information in books or on the computer to learn more. Fill in this chart.

Animal	Bird	Mammal	Reptile	Amphibian	Fish	Carnivore	Omnivore	Herbivore	Describe its habitat—Type and location	Interesting fact #1	Interesting fact #2

Worksheet

The United States of America

Label the states. Color the map.

Worksheet

Great Beginnings

Worksheet

Can you identify the following patriotic words? They are the beginning words of different songs, speeches, or documents vital to the history of the United States. If you don't recognize them, do some research to find the answers.

Answer Box

"America the Beautiful"
Bill of Rights
Constitution
Declaration of Independence
Gettysburg Address
"The Star-Spangled Banner"

1. When in the Course of human events, it becomes necessary for one people to dissolve the political bands which have connected them with another . . .

   ____

2. O beautiful for spacious skies, For amber waves of grain,
   For purple mountain majesties . . .

   ____

3. Oh! say, can you see, by the dawn's early light,
   What so proudly we hailed at the twilight's last gleaming? . . .

   ____

4. We the people of the United States, in order to form a more perfect Union, establish justice, insure domestic tranquility, provide for the common defense . . .

   ____

5. Congress shall make no law respecting an establishment of religion, or prohibiting the free exercise thereof; or abridging the freedom of speech . . .

   ____

6. Four score and seven years ago our fathers brought forth upon this continent a new nation, conceived in liberty, and dedicated to the proposition that all men are created equal. Now we are engaged in a great civil war . . .

   ____

Fifth Grade Life

Worksheet

What was life like for fifth graders 50 years ago? Interview a grandparent or an elderly friend or neighbor to find out.

Step 1
Think of questions you could ask. Write your four favorite ones here.

____

____

____

____

Step 2
Decide whom you would like to interview. Will you meet in person or will you need to conduct a phone interview for someone out of town? Politely ask the person if you may conduct an interview. Set up a date and time.

Person ____________________ Date ____________ Time __________

Step 3
Prepare your materials. Organize your questions on another sheet of paper with room to write answers. Decide if you would also like to tape record or videotape the interview and gather what you need.

Step 4
Conduct your interview. If you think of other questions, ask them. Be willing to share information about what fifth grade life is like for you. Be sure to thank the person when the interview is over.

Step 5
Read over the questions and answers. Make a Venn diagram that compares fifth grade life for you and the person you interviewed. In the area where the ovals overlap, write similarities. In the other spaces, list details about differences. Share your completed diagram with the person you interviewed.

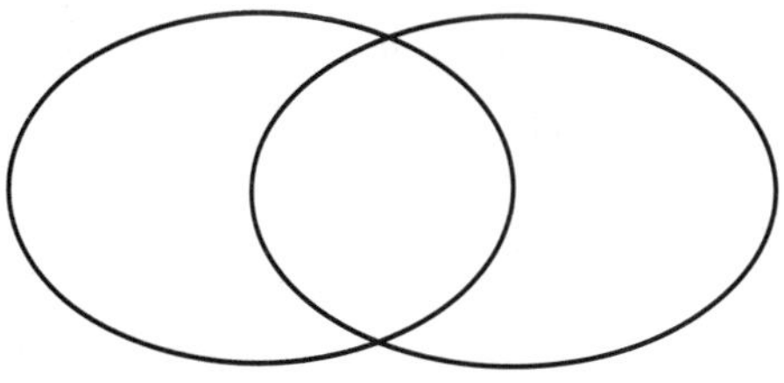

Watercolor Weaving

Worksheet

Try this painting and weaving project.

Materials:

8-inch square of white paper
watercolors
scissors
glue
9" x 12" colored construction paper
yarn and string (optional)

Directions:

1. Using the watercolors, paint colorful swirls and shapes all over the white square of paper.
2. Let the paint dry. Then cut the square into approximately half-inch wide strips.
3. Apply glue to only one end of half the strips. Glue them side by side on the colored construction paper, leaving about a half inch of space between each strip. Let the glue dry.
4. One by one, weave each of the remaining strips through the first strips. Glue both ends of these strips to the colored paper once the weaving is complete. (Optional: Weave different thicknesses and textures of yarn and string in between the strips of paper for added interest.)
5. Glue down the other end of the first strips.
6. Your watercolor weaving is ready for framing!

Musical Mysteries

Worksheet

For a treble clef, use the phrase *Every Good Boy Does Fine* to remember the letter names of the lines from bottom to top. The letter names of the spaces spell the word *FACE.*

Write the letter names of the notes on the staffs below. If you are correct, the names will spell a word.

Active and Passive

Worksheet

Some activities require energy and provide exercise. These activities are **active**. Other activities do not require much movement or use of energy. These are **passive**. Although rest and relaxation are important, strong, healthy bodies need exercise and fresh air. Study the list of activities below. Classify them using the following code.

A – active
P – passive
I – usually done indoors
O – usually done outdoors
WT – would like to try
HT – have tried

1. baseball ____________
2. football ____________
3. softball ____________
4. swimming ____________
5. jogging ____________
6. biking ____________
7. tennis ____________
8. table tennis ____________
9. ice skating ____________
10. reading ____________
11. stamp collecting ____________
12. hiking ____________
13. camping ____________
14. cards ____________
15. board games ____________
16. television ____________
17. birdwatching ____________
18. musical instrument ____________
19. downhill skiing ____________
20. x-country skiing ____________
21. fishing ____________
22. video games ____________
23. painting ____________
24. photography ____________
25. karate ____________
26. gymnastics ____________
27. ballet ____________
28. canoeing ____________

Record your activities for a week. Create a chart like this. Indicate the date and the amount of time you spent at each activity. Mark whether the activity is active or passive.

Date	Activity	Minutes	Active	Passive

What Would You Do?

Worksheet

Most situations can be handled in different ways. It is up to us to decide at the time which way is best. For each situation below, cross out the least appropriate solution.

1. You bought a new video game and don't want to share it.
   - A. Take it on the bus and tell everyone your parents won't let you share it.
   - B. Leave it at home and play with it when you are alone.

2. The new student is in a wheelchair.
   - A. Invite the student to join your game and ask which position he or she would like to try.
   - B. Avoid asking the student to join in games because it might embarrass him or her.
3. A stranger calls for your parents when you are home alone.
   - A. Tell the caller that your parents aren't home and take a message.
   - B. Tell the caller that your parents can't come to the phone and take a message.
4. You find a bottle of medicine on the sidewalk.
   - A. Read the directions carefully before trying it.
   - B. Give it to an adult immediately.
5. You heard something very scary on the news.
   - A. Talk to someone you trust that can help you understand it.
   - B. Don't tell anyone because they will think you are a big baby.
6. You notice someone picking on your friend.
   - A. Walk up to your friend and say, "Come on, let's go."
   - B. Pretend you don't see it so the bully doesn't bother you, too.

Read each of these situations. Role play them with a friend or family member. See how differently each turns out depending on how you handle it.

- Your friends are playing ball without you.
- Your mom made up a new family rule that you disagree with.
- Your little brother mixed up all your baseball cards.
- You found a wallet on the floor at school.
- You found a pack of cigarettes.

You Set the Pace

Worksheet

Do you have trouble getting moving in the morning? Does someone need to keep prodding you along to get you out the door on time with your hair combed, teeth brushed, and both shoes tied? Design your own schedule for a morning routine and try it for one week. See if it helps.

Circle each item that is a part of your morning routine. Arrange them in order in the schedule below. Add any others that are not mentioned. Estimate and fill in the time you think you should begin each activity. Put your schedule in a convenient place and check off each item as you complete it.

Get out of bed.	Get dressed.	Eat breakfast.	Take vitamins.
Make the bed.	Brush teeth.	Brush hair.	Make your lunch.
Feed a pet.	Finish homework.	Do morning chores.	________________
Pack backpack.	Say good-bye.	________________	________________

Time	Activity	Mon.	Tues.	Wed.	Thur.	Fri.